Learning To Kiss

Eve E. Megargel

Copyright © 2016 by Eve E. Megargel

ISBN 978-1-4958-0899-9 Hardcover
ISBN 978-1-4958-1001-5 Paperback
LCCN: 2016901417

Published March 2016

INFINITY PUBLISHING
1094 New DeHaven Street, Suite 100
West Conshohocken, PA 19428-2713
Toll-free (877) BUY BOOK
Local Phone (610) 941-9999
Fax (610) 941-9959
Info@buybooksontheweb.com
www.buybooksontheweb.com

To Billy

Contents

Foreword

By Timothy M. Buie, MD
Director of Gastroenterology and Nutrition
Lurie Center for Autism, Massachusetts General
Hospital for Children

The story a doctor hears from a patient is often a collection of experiences. Patients try to describe how they feel, where exactly is the trouble, when does it happen. They want to know: How can their problem be alleviated?

Billy has continually communicated his needs, his worries, his pain, and his sadness but in ways that the listener (including myself) could not easily interpret. This is the universal experience of autism, but not only of autism. It is also often the experience of other neurological disorders that impact communication. Billy's most significant problem was not his lack of effort or capability to communicate; it was our interpretation of his messages.

In *Learning to Kiss*, Eve Megargel demonstrates this communication problem with a memoir of everyday life and some life-and-death episodes, as well. It is a familiar life for some who have experience with autism. It is also an experience that everyone should hear and understand. Told as a collection of moments in his life, we come to know Billy and the challenges that range from autism and communication impairment to a list of health issues that threaten his own life and the safety of his family and caregivers.

In this story, mistakes and missteps occur. But even with the mistakes, Billy forgave our inability to do right by him at times. He seemed always to know who was trying to do right by him. Even when things were communicated poorly, even when things were difficult, he persevered. To this day Billy continues to rise above any adversity he faces.

This book is an accounting of the times we fail our patients in medicine but offers guidance on how to do better. It is an accounting of the failings of education for children and adults with autism but offers observations on different solutions. It is an accounting of how families and friends often think of individuals with disabilities. It shows us ways we are insensitive but moves us to become more sensitive.

This collection of moments from Billy's life and his family's experiences paints a portrait of what daily life entails with autism in the home. It shares the sadness and struggles but also the joys and successes in a life. There is a progressive discovery of the wonderful young man hidden by his inability to tell us about himself. We see how he is able to discover himself over time.

Autism is a powerful burden on an individual. This author-mother has made that crystal clear. She has also shown that there are additional burdens to bear, including common associated medical issues that could be treated, if recognized.

Billy has had the great fortune of having an observant and thoughtful family, loved ones who are certain that a different Billy would emerge if we would only hear his messages. He has had a caring community of teachers and staff who created a stable place for him. He has had a persistent group of medical providers sticking with him through his multiple and varied ordeals. Everyone was willing to try again. Autism is not a terminal event. We continue to live with autism. In a lifetime, we have opportunities to revisit our ideas about a problem and do better with the added perspectives from our mistakes. Because of Billy, we have all become better at what we do.

Billy has hung in there with all of us. I know him as a talented artist and a happy young man who has accomplished so much. He learned to point, he learned to paint, he learned to communicate, and he learned to kiss. He is now the teacher.

Dear Reader,

My son Billy, who is now twenty-five, was diagnosed at the age of two with autism. The news was sobering and baffling. My tow-headed, beautiful, playful child began to change right before my eyes. Billy's developmental skills plummeted. Suddenly nonverbal, Billy lacked the ability to point or imitate. His sensory system was either unresponsive or over responsive. Unable to modulate his adrenaline, Billy suffered from chronic sleep deprivation. As a child, Billy was besieged by severe allergies. Mysterious rashes laced his torso and limbs. No professional could explain their origin. As an adolescent, his physical body unraveled further, with chronic digestive problems and excruciating, unexplained pain. Over the past twenty-plus years his medical issues continued to emerge, all acute, leaving Billy in a state of constant medical crisis.

But Billy learned to point. He learned to imitate. He has developed into a strong and agile athlete. Indeed, he has always been a bellwether to his adversity. Tough, resilient, and engaged, Billy has also learned how to communicate with those whom he loves, patiently observing and struggling to understand and be understood.

As an artist, Billy's exuberance for music and uncanny eye for selection and placement of paint colors on large canvasses amaze us. He works like a master, never wavering even in his darkest moments. Billy's charisma, passion, tenderness, and intensity of dynamic proportions are present every day, alongside the equally intense anger and pain.

All of these—all of who Billy is and will be—defy his diagnosis of severe autism. And it is this defiance that has compelled me to write this book.

I don't have a choice. I cannot walk around in the world as if none of this ever happened. For too many years, Billy and I, and our family, have lived alongside him in never-pausing uncertainty, suffering, and struggle. We also have experienced joy, humor, and tenderness. And that is our mutual reality.

So now I write to affirm and celebrate our lives. Years of chaos and pain cannot quell the fact that Billy's life remains a rich tapestry of relationships grounded in communication, trust, and respect. This stands in contrast to many assumptions about those profoundly impacted by autism. Billy discovered communication, and without it, Billy's health and human spirit could have been jeopardized and the quality of his life reduced to skeletal remains. It is a precipice that I do not want other families and their loved ones to face.

Learning to Kiss is Billy's story. And it is everyone's story. Each day as human beings we learn to connect and reconnect by sight, touch, taste, smell, and sound. No one wants to be rendered mute. We all want what Billy wants: the opportunity to receive and express the kiss.

Sincerely,
Eve Megargel

Prologue

December 2007

There is barely a flake on the Starbucks parking lot. I order a Christmas-blend nonfat latte and go to the car and get situated for the typically forty-five minute ride to Billy's school. The streets are clear so I decide to take Boston's Route 128. I've traveled this route since Billy was three years old. It is December 2007 and Billy has recently turned 18. Billy is at school with David, his longtime friend and speech-and-language therapist. The air is crisp and the first dangling snowflakes add a certain childlike expectation to the pending holiday season. I give myself over an hour to arrive and pick up Billy for the ride home.

I can't explain how quickly things changed. In one moment, I'm in automatic pilot, listening to NPR, and in the next moment I'm in a gridlock mess with snow flying haywire. No car is moving on the four-lane highway. It's as if a panic has ensued and everybody in the greater Boston area has decided to get a head start home. On the highway, the snow accumulation is minimal. I don't understand why we can barely move. Two hours pass and I'm only halfway to the Route 109 exit. I see people putting their cars in park so that they can pee.

I call the classroom and talk to David. He says that he will stay with Billy. All students and school personnel have been dismissed. Save for the janitor, Billy, David and his classroom teacher, the school is deserted. The halls are dark and Billy sits on a beanbag in the classroom watching the snow swirls. Through his communication device Billy asks David where Mom is. David reassures him that she is late and will be there soon. I can hear their conversation. I hang up the phone relieved that David is with Billy.

As the third hour passes, I crawl off Route 128 and take the 109 exit. The snow is now coming down at an even faster clip. Visibility is a snow-and-windswept blur. The roads are not plowed. I can't see the dividing line on the road. It is four in the afternoon and it is getting dark. Gripping the wheel, I'm stunned by the complete transformation of the environment. The road is treacherous.

This fall Billy has become increasingly uncomfortable, showing mounting distress. Trapped in the car, I'm worried that the medications I have with me will not be administered to Billy in time. I don't know what that means. Billy is volatile. He clears his throat constantly. He stares off as if he is not with us.

For the past year, Billy has exhibited an array of odd physical acts. Vomiting randomly after finishing a meal went on for a year and then stopped. Two other episodes occurred within the past school year. As if he wanted to be released from his body, Billy suddenly screamed and fled the classroom, running nowhere and lying on the cement floor banging his head as others screamed. It never happened again. But he still is not stable. As an intern in the recycling department at Crotched Mountain School, Billy completes the tasks in a professional manner. But after lunch, he runs his hands all over his head as if something is amiss. He manipulates his facial muscles, pressing the sides of his face forward to the farthest point the skin will move. After lunch, he sits with a coat over his head and nods off. None of these actions connect. They come and go like snowflakes falling on wet ground. Instinctively I'm on alert, but I don't know what to do.

I cannot be this late. If he misses his medication, I worry that Billy's anxiety will rise. I'm not concerned about the snowstorm. I'm in the eye of the storm. But it is Billy that I'm focused on. His physical health seems way too precarious. The moments when he feels well are dwindling.

Four hours later I drive up to the front doors of the school. Billy is waiting inside. When my car comes to a halt, the doors fly open. Billy is ready to go. I am relieved to see him in one piece. I give him his medicines there in the parking lot and get back in the car.

In order to avoid the clogged highways, we drive home on the back roads. It is pitch black and there are few light posts on these rural roads, which are unplowed and slippery. Billy and I are together. I am so relieved. We still have to get home. I am tense. Billy is quiet. Darkness envelops us. Dinner will be past eight p.m tonight. The radio plays the top hits.

Part One:
The Early Years

Billy was born in late November 1989. He was a beautiful, tow-headed baby. He was joyous, happy, and energetic. Nothing was remarkable . . .

Billy's First Birthday
November 1990

Sitting on my lap in the kitchen that evening, Billy snuggles and slurps his bottle. Even though he is one year old, Billy still smells like a fresh baby. Birthday cheers, presents ripping, wrapping paper, edible bakery-cake roses swallowed whole, and his brother Ben's four-year-old shrieks of delight at every crafted stage of the party: Billy is saturated. Content, his cheeks glow a "to-die-for" rosy pink as he nestles in my arms. Topping off his bottle, Billy wiggles down to the tile floor and then deftly climbs up and stands on another chair facing Matt and me. It is his first birthday and he prepares to deliver his thank-you speech. Although we are not privy to a translator for babble language, it is clear that Billy knows what he speaks. The cadence never falters. The intonations are declarative. The body language is in sync. Billy clearly speaks Chinese. That's what I said to Matt as we feasted our eyes on our one-year-old wunderkind.

Trapeze Artist
Summer 1991

Billy is a trapeze artist. Almost two, he jumps, runs, ducks, pivots, and soars through space. Every waking moment, Billy is a daredevil with boundless energy and a disarming smile. One morning at the break of dawn I hear a scuffle and immediately look into his bedroom. Before I'm able to interpret the scene, Billy scales the rail of his white crib and hoists himself on the top of the rail. The launch pad is narrow and awkward. Billy's balance and timing is impeccable. With an athlete's confidence and concentration, he leaps off the top of the banister and lands on his feet. The landing is clean. No wavering. No hands on the floor. No butt to the floor. In a gymnastics competition, I'd give it a ten. That night I relay the story to Matt. We both agree it reminded us of the legendary story of my Grandpa Edwards, a versatile athlete, former football coach, and college athletic director. Well into his sixth decade, Grandpa was cleaning the upstairs window and leaned too far out. While falling out of the window, Grandpa performed a somersault in mid-air and landed on his feet. Not a mark on him. Just one for the family record books. Matt and I nod proudly. Billy has inherited Grandpa's physical panache. It's exciting, but we still have to get the gates up.

Retrieval
February 1992

Running down the narrow front hallway of our colonial home, Billy's wispy blonde hair catches the light. Attired in an off-white, hooded, cable-ribbed cotton sweater, he looks up at me with an earnest expression of purposeful intention. Bending down to meet him, we are face to face. I cannot remember the exact words Billy uttered. I do, however, remember the implacable sense of self-awareness illuminated in his blue eyes as he paused, searched, and then retrieved the word. Silence, and then he was off like a flash. This Kodak moment is indelibly imprinted in my mind. I wish I could remember the words.

Holding Hands

It is April in Boston. The sun is shining but the air is still brisk. The buds are on the trees but there is no foliage. Each of us holding his tender,, padded, two-year-old hands, we walk as a threesome down the path to the suburban Children's Hospital satellite in Lexington. I'm not anxious about our appointment. Neither is Matt. Billy is healthy. But all the single words he has been using to label his world have suddenly disappeared. I'm just relieved we are meeting with medical professionals who can give us guidance. Matt and I want to help Billy.

Once we reach the vestibule, we are greeted by a clinician who invites us into her office. Billy sits on the floor and observes the new toys. He is content. The clinician proceeds to document Billy's medical history by asking us a series of questions. The questions are predictable. When did we first notice a decline in speech production? I inform the speech and language clinician that I had reported to our pediatrician that Billy seemed to hesitate when he spoke words. I noted that Billy was not putting words into phrases. The pediatrician scheduled hearing tests and told me to keep a journal of his language gains. A month later, I went back to Billy's pediatrician and informed her that Billy had made no progress in his speech production. Billy was losing the words he knew and said.

As I convey this information, the clinician's demeanor changes instantly. I note her concerned expression but I am not upset. In the late 1980s—and into the early 90s—there were no reference points for autism. As an adult, my only association with the word derived from the movie, *Rain Man*. A Hollywood movie about such an odd character had no bearing on my understanding of Billy. I made no connection. The questions continued. Did Billy meet the other developmental milestones? Was Billy full term? Were there any problems associated with labor or birth? The information we provide is factual and non- threatening. From our perspective, all our answers indicate that there are no flashpoints.

Then the question-and-answer period ends and the clinician sits down on the floor next to Billy. Matt and I stay in chairs that encircle their play area. The clinician makes repeated attempts to engage

Billy. Her initiatives are friendly, warm, and inviting. But Billy does not respond. He seems almost preoccupied. Disconnected. The Billy we know is missing. Neither Matt nor I have ever viewed Billy as withdrawn. At home he is buoyant, full of physical and emotional vitality. But in that medical office, Matt and I see Billy as utterly different. It is as if our eyes have betrayed us and now, in this moment, we see a new Billy. An unknown Billy. As we gather our belongings and walk back together holding hands, we would never be the same family. Now we would work hard to regain our confidence in Billy and ourselves. Perhaps T.S. Eliot is right when he characterized April as the cruelest month of all.

It's All in the Delivery

After our initial screening with the clinician in Lexington, it is advised that Billy undergo a comprehensive review by a team of developmental specialists from various disciplines. A month later on a Friday afternoon, we drive into Boston Children's Hospital for a presentation of each member's' findings and the team's overarching conclusions about Billy.

We think that we will meet with members of the team who did the assessments. But that is not the case. Upon learning that no one from the actual assessment team will be there, I am incensed. Instinctively my guard goes up. This important meeting is with an individual we have never met. She doesn't know Billy. She doesn't know us.

We are escorted into a cramped interior room by a cardiac emergency-room nurse who claims that she meets with parents concerning their children's reviews. Her presence seems like an invasion of our family's privacy. The meeting is a drone of details covering the different specialists' reports.

In mid-stream, the cardiac nurse reports that the team concurs that Billy's diagnosis is Pervasive Developmental Disorder, more commonly referred to as PDD. She adds that Billy has enough deficits in the majority of the documented developmental categories that render such a diagnosis. She emphasizes that Billy is too young to conclude that autism will be the final diagnosis. The term PDD, however, will assure that Billy receives a full array of therapeutic services. Hearing the word "autism" associated with Billy's PDD status is confusing. Is the label PDD a way to explain to my friends and family what is happening to Billy without condemning Billy to the murky world of autism?

Now I am on high alert. I know that the essence of the word "pervasive" means "everywhere". I am alarmed. But more, I am angry that a total stranger feels so comfortable using such a damning word to depict Billy. Her review reads like a defamation.

I cannot listen anymore. I interrupt her litany of clinical signs and demand to know what exactly "pervasive" means in this medical context. Calmly, she refers to the total number of composite checks as determining the final conclusion. I still don't comprehend what pervasive means for Billy. Her answer is sobering. Her answer tells us nothing. Her answer is laden with hopelessness. After all, Billy's diagnosis reads PDD, or Pervasive Developmental Disorder. Sensing our rising tension she wraps up our meeting with one final statement. Through education, improvement is possible, but it will be very hard work. Hard work is emphasized multiple times. That is it. No mention of a follow-up meeting. No mention of resources. Just a solid handshake.

It is not an acceptable answer. This official report is based on observations, not hard science. Billy is not the summation of these categorical checkpoints. No one is. What is missing from this medical analysis is that regardless of the obstacles, Billy is an individual with a family and ancestry that cannot be summarily underestimated or dismissed. Like any two year old, Billy's story is in its infancy. There were, are, and will be so many transformations. The data cannot account for those other human qualities that alter the playing field.

That late Friday afternoon Matt and I walk out of our meeting and curtly thank the cardiac nurse for her time. The hospital seems deserted. It is June and there are few true summer weekends left. In silence we walk to the garage and in silence we sit in the car and stare straight ahead. This is a silence born out of grief. This is a silence born out of our uncontestable resolve. We know it will be the hardest walk of our lives but we also know that Billy will prevail. It is his birthright.

We don't want to go home. So we go to the movies. A summer blockbuster movie is showing. At least sitting in the dark provides a temporary salve. As the movie ends we run into one of Matt's business partners. Matt works closely with him every day, but as he shakes the man's hand he seems at a loss. He can't remember his name. Startled by his lack of command, I put my hand out and state my name. It is an awkward moment.

I Thought I was Okay

I thought I was okay. Yes, initially the news was shell shocking. But I thought I was okay. Billy is a robust, healthy two-year old whose energy, coordination, charm, and affection are brilliance in motion. I know my Billy. No diagnosis will ever alter his dynamic soul. We will work hard, forge ahead, and resume our lives. Our plan is to get up Saturday morning and drive to Crane's Beach in Ipswich. The June weekend forecast predicts a clear, sunny, and warm day. It is a perfect family outing. Chasing the boys up and down the beach, digging sand fortresses, and luxuriating in the sun will be the quintessential antidote. That's how the scenario played out in my mind. It was, however, only part of my reality.

It is only a week after our meeting with the cardiac nurse. The diagnosis of PDD impacts everyone in the family. I am no exception.

As the light streams into our bedroom, my eyes open sluggishly but my senses pulsate wildly. Sitting up abruptly in bed, I peer at myself in the gilded-frame mirror hanging above the dresser directly in front of our bed. I no longer look like myself. I am no longer Eve. My face, grotesquely swollen and intensely red, vibrates. I cannot will this repugnant image away. My body, the soothsayer speaks. With an extra wide sombrero-style hat and Dior-style black shades, I shield my throbbing face from the blazing sun. I am incognito. It will not be the first time or the last. My public persona is my shield. It is also Billy's first defense. Billy cannot speak and now, neither can I.

The freedom to discuss autism is not yet possible. Stereotypes are rampant. Prejudice is pervasive. On that hot summer day, the floppy-brimmed sunhat shielding my bloated face is all I have.

Circle Time Shutdown

Billy received the diagnosis of Pervasive Developmental Disorder in June, but will not turn three until the end of November. So there are no official school-related services available until the upcoming year. Billy and I are in therapy limbo. After a persuasive appeal, Billy is referred by the Boston Children's Hospital developmental team to begin a speech-and-language class located on the hospital premises.

Fighting commuter traffic, Billy and I hustle to the 9:30 a.m. class two days a week. The class is composed of five children exhibiting a cadre of different communication disorders. It is a cheerful place with a serious mission. At the end of each session, the teacher concludes with a circle time filled with songs, colorful props, and merriment. All the children are engaged except Billy. Billy cradles himself on the floor between my knees. It is a cozy but tight space. Billy's eyes glaze over. His head bobs and then nods on his chest. Billy's eyes close and his mouth is slack. His body leans into my gut. Billy is motionless. In this child-friendly and stimulating environment, Billy is uncomfortable. The more language directed at him, the more he retreats.

Sleep seems to be his only refuge. It is not mine. Billy's quiet withdrawal stimulates my senses. I cannot rest. My nights are sleepless. During those silent dark hours, I read firsthand accounts of others' experiences with loving a child with autism. I feel so ill prepared. But there is no retreat. When circle time ends, I put Billy in his stroller. Asleep, his body is limp and sweet. Entering the elevator, we encounter a therapist from the assessment team. She smiles, says hello, and asks how things are going. I smile and deliver the "fine" answer. Billy never saw her. Billy never heard her. Billy is in shutdown and I am the only one who sees it. I am taking all the right intervention measures and nothing seems to be working.

Boston Children's Hospital – Fall 1992

Speech and Language class at Boston Children's Hospital begins at 9:30 a.m. Billy and I head toward the city on Route 9, which is a sluggish nightmare commute. My stress mounts. We hustle, arrive, and sit abruptly down at the play table together. There are no normal transitions for me or for Billy. That day the town preschool special-needs coordinator is present to observe. She is behind a glass booth that enables visitors a bird's-eye view. The special-needs coordinator thinks it is advisable that I join her in the soundproof booth. From her perspective, Billy needs social interaction time with others. It is true that I am the only parent in this cramped, borderline-claustrophobic room. But Billy is the only child who does not speak.

With grave reservations, I leave and join her. But it is not easy. Billy screams, howls, and sobs uncontrollably. Red welts mark his face as his tears fall fast and hard. As the teacher beams and stacks the colorful blocks, she tries valiantly to distract Billy from dwelling on my absence. Unperturbed, the teacher fashions her fingertips together in the symbol for "more" and sweetly asks Billy if he would like "more" blocks. There is no response. Billy cannot mimic. She repeats the question. Billy cannot comprehend her melodious words. Determined to stay on task, she demonstrates again the sign for more and repeats the question. His belly-laden wallows fall on deaf ears. Cast in a room full of strangers who speak a language that he can't decipher, Billy fights like hell to be heard.

This version of playtime is not the answer. Why would it be? Billy has no idea where I am. No words can explain to Billy that I'm right around the corner and that I'll be right back. I cannot use words to reassure Billy as he sees me stand and walk away from him. My departure unravels him and no one understands. No one is perturbed by Billy's passionate outburst. It doesn't matter to them. The communication objective is to sign for "more".

I hear him through the walls. Unable to listen anymore, I stand up and inform the coordinator that this isn't working. I walk back into the room and tightly gather Billy in my arms. The remainder of the sessions I never leave his side. Extricating me so that Billy will interact and learn from others how to communicate doesn't work. It achieves the opposite. Fear of the unknown elicits retreat.

I'm not sure Billy ever really benefited from the sessions that fall. No matter how rambunctious, musical, or theatrical the activity, Billy remained at best aloof. When circle time concluded each session with joyful singing, Billy closed his eyes, bowed his head, and slept in my lap. At the time, I didn't know why Billy retreated. I only knew that I too felt his fear of the communication abyss.

Finger Painting

As a young child, I loved everything about finger painting. There were the bright colors. There was the feel of the slippery paint coating my fingers. There was the gliding of my hands in every direction across the large white paper. There were no rules. There were no guidelines. It was pure chaos. I felt so free. I felt so happy as a child.

So when Lori, the speech therapist, suggests that we try finger painting as a joint activity with Billy, I think this a marvelous idea. It is autumn and Billy has almost three more months to wait for the school services to begin, so I continue to find other ways to stimulate Billy to interact in all mediums. Everything will be set up and ready to go. It is a confusion-free activity.

As I take Billy's hands and guide them through the paint and on to paper, he screams at the top of his lungs. The origin of his scream is primal. His face turns burnt red. I try again and Billy recoils at the mere touch of the paint on his little hands. I am both witness to and instigator of a complete sensory misfire in his toddler frame. Picking him up, I hoist him on the side of my body and lunge toward the nearest sink. The paint has to be removed. In a frenzied state, I wash and wipe all paint remnants off of Billy's hands. In synchronized time, I pour the remaining paint cups into the drain. The sink is cleaned. The paint is put away. Out of sight. Billy calms down. My mind is blank. Billy's rapid-fire response of total dissolution to such a beloved childhood activity unnerves me. It is another shutdown. It is another dead end.

Billy Didn't Die

Matt snores peacefully. Billy and Ben are asleep. It is two in the morning and I am awake. I take my book and a Waterford glass of Maker's Mark and tiptoe into the sitting room next to our bedroom. I look for answers every night in the dark. Books have always been my refuge and now I read Clarissa Claiborne Park's book, *The Siege*. It is about her life with her daughter who has autism. It is about the family. My late reads are a quest to understand what I cannot grasp. Sleep is no longer a sanctuary. My fears infiltrate my dreams, but this particular dream causes my body's sensations to surface and tingle throughout my central nervous system. Startled, I awake as if someone has broken into the house. In the dream, I am in my childhood home and I have a tiger on a leash. I do not want to keep it. I search for my father but to no avail. In the morning I name my emotion. Fear.

The following day, it is late afternoon. Billy giggles, runs, and dances with Ben to the soul sounds of Tina Turner. The phone rings as I sit on the couch watching the boys' antics. It is a long-distance telephone call. My mother is in Cleveland Heights and I am in Boston. The distance, however, is insignificant. Grief envelops us. It overwhelms me. It overwhelms my mother. Yet I cannot stay in a perpetual wake. All the doctors, teachers, therapists, neighbors, and strangers believe that Billy is no longer the little boy I see playing with Ben. On some level, the clinical view is absurd. But having a child that cannot speak is unthinkable.

For Billy, language or the freedom to express oneself in words won't happen. That's why I am on the phone long distance to Ohio. Neither my mother nor I can imagine a world stripped of words. I know Billy will never speak. I call it gut knowledge. My mother holds out. She speaks to me of dreams where Billy is present and speaks to her. "Mom, Billy didn't die. Billy is with us." My declaration, however, is not the whole truth. The pauses on each side of the line are mournful. Tearfully, my mother agrees. Locked in a state of grief, we both struggle to understand a mute Billy.

It is a phone call I will never forget. I'm not afraid of the tiger. I do not seek shelter. I seek answers and that day I knew that whatever language system Billy used, it would be mine as well. Tina Turner, Billy and Ben, and self-expression will unfold.

Wake Up Call

It is our first meeting with the out-of-district coordinator for special education. We are in her office to find out what educational services Billy will receive at the age of three. Although highly educated, neither Matt nor I understand from a curriculum standpoint what constitutes a special education. We are here to listen and learn. Our only aim is that Billy receives the highest-quality education. Nothing less.

Matt and I listen carefully as she enumerates the legal rights and mandated services related to Billy's diagnosis of Pervasive Developmental Disorder. The special-education laws and mandates are all consuming. Our allotted meeting time is almost finished. No mention yet of Billy. No mention of how we will help Billy. No mention of how the school system will help Billy. At almost three years old, Billy neither speaks nor understands verbal directions, comments, or questions. He does not respond to his own name. Billy understands nothing. We have yet to reach Billy. As his anxiety, frustration, and fears mount, so does ours.

It is clear that Billy is not viewed as a learner. I'm not sure why we are here. It feels like a mock trial. The judge and jury have already arrived at a verdict and now it's just about finalizing the paperwork. This is not an educational meeting. As the meeting concludes, she offers us her number-one goal for Billy. Unabashedly she declares that, "Bill needs to learn to comply."

So the summation of Billy's education is deemed obedience. Without a breath, I whip back my answer.

"No, Billy needs to learn to communicate."

Neither one of us concedes.

This is no longer a philosophical debate. This debate about the course of Billy's education—compliance versus communication—will be at the crux of every dialogue and every impasse. In that moment nobody could have predicted that communication would later become a lifeline for Billy as he navigated the medical matrix.

Digging a Hole at Skaket Beach

In order to take Billy to the beach, I must dig a hole. It is low tide and I need to work fast before Billy waivers. Buckets of moist sand are dumped around the perimeters as the space deepens and is wide enough for Billy to sit in. The walled sand fortress is a temporary buffer to the unwieldy beach landscape. Billy feels safer seated underground. The assault of the light and the movement of the ocean mass are less threatening. I open a low-to-the-ground beach chair and plop my body right next to Billy. The sun is warm and inviting. The air and water are salty. I hand him some Cheerios from the Ziploc bag. Framed by a sand excavation and in silhouette relief, Billy and I become part of the beach scene. A day at the beach rarely happens.

Swinging
Summer 1993

Billy is fearless. He loves the arched height of the swing as it moves upward and backward. Feet up! Feet down! My vocalized commands accompany every single motion. Billy's legs haltingly lift up and barely sway back. It is not easy. It is not instinctive. Swinging must be taught. Swinging up and down is my mantra. I don't analyze it. I don't count the number of times I have or will utter those words. Feet Up! Feet down! It doesn't work that way. High expectations are grounded in faith.

Billy at the Horse Stable

It's a cloudy cool autumn day in New England. It is late afternoon. The days are shorter and soon it will be dusk. It is Billy's turn for his weekly therapeutic horseback riding session. The instructor beams at Billy as she takes his toddler hand and moves it toward the ring of pictures that I've made and specifically points to the word "Go". Attentive to Billy and the card a volunteer holds, she commands the horse to "Go". The horse obliges and ambles forward. Billy in his bobbling black helmet sits erect on the horse, inert yet coiled. Then Billy grinds his teeth audibly, clenches the saddle knob and forces his vocal chords to wail punctuated tones of dissent. Lurching his body forward as if to lay prostrate on the horse's back, Billy places his crimson cheek down on the woven blanket draped over the horse. He now lies very still, attuned to the horse's pulse, in unison with his own as they jaunt around the earth-baked practice ring. The lesson concludes and the horse halts at the designated place to dismount. With guidance from his teacher, Billy deftly glides down the side of the horse and in lightning speed jams the carrot toward the horse's mouth. Billy jerks the helmet off his head and leaves it spinning. I'm not sure that Billy likes anything about horseback riding.

But I know why we go. On the eve of darkness, I follow Billy. Without a cue, Billy walks into the cavernous, dimly lit stable and peers through a chicken-wire fence with a narrow gape in the mesh. Billy places his compact hand just inside the wired opening and waves to the physically regal work horse that stands inches away. Face to face, Billy and the horse stand. The only sounds are the nostril breath noises of the horse, the rustle of hay, and the smells of the manure, mud, and rotting leaves. His hand wiggles in between the slats. With his hooded back to the world, Billy waves just slightly and off center to the proud old horse. Every week in the musty horse stall, Billy makes connections.

Chicken Pox

The hot blisters cover the inside of his throat, his nose, his eyelids, and his ears. Ben is just recovering from the chicken pox. And now ten days later, it's Billy's turn. This time, however, I'm alarmed. Maybe it's the fact that Ben at the age of six is three years older and can tell me how he feels and where it hurts. Billy cannot utter a word. Pox riddle his body. He is feverishly sick. But it is his silent anguish that unnerves me. Doing nothing is not the answer. I haul the boys in the car and head to the ever-so familiar pediatrician's office. Because we are contagious, we arrive incognito through the back door and file into an examination room. Huddled together in this cubicle space, we wait for the doctor to check the medical folder in the slot adjacent to the door and enter. I am distressed.

As a child, getting the chicken pox was not a big deal. I remember being impatient and annoyed by the final, ugly pox scab that stubbornly stuck to the middle of my forehead. My mother told me not to "pick it" because it would leave a "scar". Standing in front of the vestibule's full-length door mirror, those cautionary words of course went unheeded. Chicken pox resulted in maybe acquiring a minor scar or two and a week off from school. I just didn't recall that the chicken pox inundated your body and caused such unbridled suffering.

The doctor comes in and asks the perennial medical question: "What's wrong?" Cradling Billy in my arms with Ben enfolded into the side of my body, I summarize the obvious. Billy's version of the chicken pox is acute and his pain is intolerable. I also inform the doctor that Billy has autism, is unable to speak, and that we use visuals to facilitate greater comprehension. Nodding knowingly, the doctor responds by telling Billy to "lie down" on the examination table so she can have a "look". My relief to be finally seeing the doctor dissolves instantly. My body heat rises and my cheeks and throat flush red. In disbelief, I take another look at her. Does she not hear me? Does she not believe me? Does she not understand? Have I also been rendered mute?

Uncomfortably angry, I repeat the pertinent information: "Billy cannot understand you." Taken aback by the gravity of my declaration, the doctor appears uncertain about how to proceed. We stumble through the exam. It is perfunctory. There are no conclusions drawn. There are no questions asked. Chicken pox is understood. Autism is not.

It doesn't seem right. Billy neither speaks nor follows specific verbal commands. His body is covered with pox and he is scared. I am scared. Healing will not commence in the doctor's office.

The Look

It's an expectant look. It's a fleeting hunger to try. Standing on my lap, Billy stretches his neck as he watches Ben take ice-skating lessons at the Waltham MDC. From the bleachers, Billy surveys the ice turf and scrambles to his tiptoes for a better view. Intrigued by the collective movement on ice, Billy lunges forward as I hold on to his toddler legs. I know the look. It's the Billy look. So I say, "Billy, would you like to ice skate like Ben?"

There is a fiery yet playful glint in Billy eyes. The look is the blink.

Ring around the Kitchen Table

It is dinnertime for Ben and Billy. Happily, Ben takes his seat at the head of the table. Perched on his knees with his feet tucked under his bottom, Ben has a bird's-eye view of the pending, raucous pre-dinner event. On cue, bare-footed and with flushed cheeks, Billy enters the kitchen and without hesitation starts the never-ending victory lap. Ben's neck strains to keep track of Billy's whippet motions around the farm table. As Billy maneuvers the corners with hairpin-right angles, I brace myself. Billy turns the corner and I swoop down and pluck him up and in mid-air drop him on his assigned chair. Within seconds, Billy wiggles out of the seat and speeds away.

Although Billy craves the spinning motion, I will not let him be anchorless. It is dinnertime and in order to eat, one has to sit at the table. Curious and sincere, Ben asks me why Billy is running endlessly around the kitchen table. I don't know the answer. All I can think of is the chaotic scene in the book, *The Miracle Worker*. Helen Keller's teacher, Anne Sullivan, locks the doors to the dining room and wages a war of ironclad wills. Food flies. Dishes break. Physical tussle ensues. It is a bar brawl every night. There is no exit. The stakes are too high. It is also turning point in Billy's life. If Billy never learns to sit for dinner, the quality of his life deteriorates. He will never know the joy and comfort of eating and being in the company of family and friends. Billy would be literally alone. An outcast. In my struggle to teach Billy the social and physical realities of eating dinner with his brother, I do not eat dinner with Billy and Ben. I'm not hungry. I am determined. I am Billy's teacher. Ben witnesses daily the answer to his simple yet poignant question. Billy cannot find his way alone.

Nail Cutting

It is 7 p.m. Dinner is finished. Billy and I huddle in our respective corners. Crouched in the bathroom by the locked door, I hold tight the nail scissors in my hand. Billy sits in the opposite corner of the bathroom, sweating and visibly anxious. The sounds Billy makes are pitched and discordant. It is our weekly session. One fingernail at a time, Billy and I crawl barely to the middle section of the beige, marbled floor. I hold out my open hand and wait for my terrified toddler to show his hand. Billy yanks it back. His youthful face marred by kinetic fear, he retreats to his corner. He cannot do it. He wants to do it. But the sound of the nail, the sound of the scissors, and the brushing of metal on nail overpowers his understanding. His little hand edges forward slightly. It is one piece of one nail at a time. One piece of a nail repeated over and over. There is no other way. Billy must know that I will not betray his trust. I will cut his small white nails one sliver at a time.

Wind

Billy's blonde hair swirls in the crinkling autumn leaves. Mom and I frame him as we lie on the ground together. The sun is still warm and we are a content family. Billy turns his head side to side and grins at both of us. Then his gaze shifts toward the sky and the stark white clouds floating against a brilliant blue. We are all smiling. Mom remarks that Billy is such a beautiful child. As we nestle in our bed of glowing leaves, Billy stands up, turns, and opens his arms like a bird in flight. His palms are flat and open to receive. I'm not sure what he is doing and then I realize the simplicity of his action. Billy senses the wind with his supplicant hands. His senses seem so natural, grounded, and alert.

Learning to Kiss

No one ever recommends that I should teach Billy how to give and receive a kiss. No one ever thinks about it. It occurs to no one. The diagnosis of autism undermines perception. Yet the ability to kiss is a primal human act of tender connection. As a two year old, Billy cannot form the physical act of a kiss. The inability to neither speak nor express the intimate act of a kiss forces Billy into deeper social isolation.

To kiss is so effortless and so taken for granted. From the age of two to the age of six, every day and every night I kiss Billy goodnight. His mouth ajar, slightly drooling down the corners of his mouth from a jaw that the doctors conjecture as "low tone," Billy never rebukes my lesson. He seeks the closeness. With surprising delicacy, Billy moves his face towards my lips and receives. He is not ashamed of the lackluster quality of his countless attempts. There is no anxious hesitation. There is no social agenda. There is no vanity. There is pure affectionate expression. The brushing of lips is a balm. Our daily kisses transcend the constant undercurrent of aloneness, his and mine.

Part Two:
The Elementary Years

When Billy entered the public school system, his autism diagnosis limited his learning opportunities. Plagued by odd and random medical issues attributed to the severity of his autism, communication was not an educational objective to anyone—except me. This was the beginning of a long crusade to persuade teachers, doctors, nurses, and therapists to see beyond Billy's physical and developmental challenges and look at him, interact with him, and know him.

What Do You Do on the Ride to School?

"What do you do on the ride to school?" The teacher's question catches me off guard. It feels crude. The implication is barely disguised. How could one be in a relationship with a human being who does not speak? The intent is empathic curiosity. The effect, however, is jarring. I am offended and I'm not exactly sure why. It is a candid question. It is a fair question. The teacher's basic inquiry highlights the fact that Billy does not speak and that as a five year old with severe autism, Billy will never cross the divide into the realm of a language-dominated culture. In the middle of the night, I've been haunted by the prospect that Billy will remain mute. His vulnerability to every type of exploitation seeps into my every waking and somnolent moment. Francois Truffaut's film, *L'Enfant Sauvage*, also known as *The Wild Child*, darkens my interior monologue. The film underscores the commonly held notion that a young boy who cannot speak is deemed less than human: a wild child. Will Billy, my "wild child," be subject to such callous attitudes and primitive reprisals? Billy is a five year old with severe autism; I cannot look away from what lies underneath this question. My immediate thoughts are suppressed but held tight in my ever-changing emotional landscape. I pause. I smile and say that Billy and I listen to music. We enjoy our time together in the car. The teacher nods. I'm not sure she believes me. The absence of language as the human connector means there is no way to know the other. Language trumps all other senses as a viable bond.

Before Billy, I believed that without the ability to speak one could never truly be in relation with another. Every day on the twenty-five mile drive to Billy's out-of-district placement, I know that this common belief is short sighted. Our other senses are overpowered by our dependency on spoken language.

Silence is awkward. Silence conjures the fear of being disconnected. Alone.

Enveloped in our white Mercury Sable, however, Billy and I are visually acute to each other's movements, gestures, facial expressions, and intonations. Every sound and image is acknowledged. Driving Billy to school is a shared experience.

Billy's First Yes

In a grandiose style, I announce to Billy that today is his fifth birthday. Billy's tongue clicks between his lips and the roof of his mouth. I dare not believe it. The muffled click emerges from somewhere in the vicinity of his still baby-pouched lips. The sound is barely audible but I hear it. I kneel down so that Billy and I are face to face.

My thoughts race. How can Billy be a reliable source? Did I hear it? Did I just see his lips faintly part? Perhaps I am momentarily delusional. Are my anxieties about Billy's increasing vulnerability as a nonverbal person overriding my common sense? No. I never dream or daydream about Billy suddenly speaking. Never. It's been years since I've heard Billy utter a word. The last time he was two years old and it was winter. But I heard the faint click. Holding my breath I continue.

"There will be cake."

Billy clicks his tongue.

"There will be ice cream."

The sound is even stronger, bearing the tone of an exclamation mark. Billy smiles, as if he anticipates the next word.

"Presents."

Yes! He clicks again.

Now I know.

For years I announced a week in advance to Billy that soon it would be his birthday. I rattled off the list of party accoutrements he seemed to enjoy. But I never received a yes, a nod, or a pointed finger to a birthday picture. Every year at his birthday on Thanksgiving, my Happy Birthday wishes were met by my sweet little boy's silence. Curious, attentive, but mute.

Billy said yes. Now I know. Billy understood my years of daily narrations about what he was doing and what I was doing.

The door cracks open and a sliver of light peeked through. A lighthouse beam in a foggy night is my guidepost. I am relieved. I am ecstatic. I am emboldened.

Trick or Treat

Halloween is Ben's holiday. On the eve of Halloween, Billy's brother transforms himself. His voice cackles. His elbows rise and his hands claw the air. His eyebrows are penciled black and red, blood-oozing fake wounds slice his cheek. His eyeballs pop as he hisses and slithers and whips his black cape in every direction. It is no act. It is real. Ben is the vampire.

Whatever the chosen costume, Ben undergoes a complete metamorphosis. He is devilish, wicked, cagey, and always witty. But what makes his Halloween revelry so enticing are his creative passion and the glint of sheer glee in his eyes. Billy sees it, too. Even though costumes, hats, and trick or treating create a baffling sensory overload, Billy still plays along. Ben is far too seductive in his unfolding persona to be denied. So Billy puts on the green joker costume and wears the lime-green bowler hat decorated with a large white question mark strategically centered on the front. Ben cavorts and Billy grins ear to ear. Billy is the adoring audience and that's all Ben asks for.

Saturday Night Live

Billy revels in circular motion. The tire swing located in the basement recreation room is hooked up to an industrial-strength metal cable attached to the drop-tile ceiling. Every night after dinner, Ben and Billy scramble downstairs for a live music jam. Ben selects the latest pop hit and sings into his hand microphone. Ben gets top billing. Billy plays backup. Music blaring, Ben bellows out the words and gyrates trend-setting moves. Behind Ben, Billy performs his part for the night gig. Draped over the tire swing in a Superman flight pose, Billy whizzes around and around. He never takes a break. Neither does Ben. Grinning ear to ear, Billy pushes the tire swing to the edge. Ben moves seamlessly around the circumference of the ballistic tire swing with Billy at the helm. Their act is daring, theatrical, and soul gritty. What a duo!

Flasher

They never saw it coming. With lightning speed Billy streaks past them. Only the whiff of peanut butter lingers in the air. Billy is naked and covered from head to toe in peanut butter. I imagine Billy's delight when in the bathroom he unrigs the childproof lock and discovers an unopened jar of Skippy's. As far as Billy is concerned, he'd hit the jackpot and won the lottery. Nothing rates like a sensory bath of creamy peanut butter. Knowing Billy he probably licked his sticky fingers clean. This after-school program rocks!

When I arrive to collect my little flasher, he is spanking clean. He is, however, sporting a new hairstyle. Slicked back and shiny. I ask Kim, the owner of the program, about his new hairdo. And then the story unfolds.

Immediately after his peanut butter escapade, the girls went to work and put him in the bathtub. Little did they know that peanut butter and suds were now the ultimate reward. I couldn't help but smile. What a cad!

Christmas in Ohio

The staircase landing at Granny and Grandpa's three-story, 1940s home in Ohio is where Billy and Matt celebrate Christmas. The staircase is where I go, each year, to offer Matt a present for Billy. With Pavarotti's *Ave Maria* serenading all who listen, my Christmas mornings are sojourns up the staircase to the landing and then down to the other Christmas.

The other Christmas is a clan in motion. Family members rearrange furniture to accommodate the gathering pajama-clad crowd, while others strategically place their coffee cups so as not to interfere with the unveiling of the gifts. I find my niche and curl up on the white love seat next to my sister. Ben sits between his cousins Matt and Alex on the matching white sofa that together form an "L". The Christmas tree is alit with white lights reflected in the bowed and leaded-glass windows. The fireplace mantle bedecked by angel choirs and music bands, a white, stone-carved scene of the manger, and my father's childhood metal soldiers brigade accents the family's idiosyncratic festivities.

Amidst the breaks for more trips to the kitchen in search of fresh coffee and Poland Spring water, I steal away to the staircase bearing bagels with cream cheese and another present for Billy. As the pile of untouched presents stacks up around Billy, in the other room Ben and his cousins gleefully rip at the shining paper and curly ribbons and bows to find the next gift. Cousin Elizabeth, the youngest and only girl, sits on Grandpa's lap in the corner chair in safe distance from the band of boys' camaraderie. In rapt attention, Elizabeth listens to Grandpa's stage-worthy rendition of her new Christmas story. After the opening of the gifts extravaganza, Ben, Alex, and Matt sit together on Granny's white sofa raving about their booty as they stuff their mouths with Godiva chocolates from their stockings. Cooking the traditional family brunch, Granny paces back and forth from the kitchen delighting in her grandchildren's revelry. A touch bleary eyed from the Christmas Eve dinner shenanigans, the aunts and uncles spearhead the ruckus with running commentary shooting in every direction. Then one by one they head for more coffee and maybe a muffin.

Billy and Matt sit on the last step of the staircase. Christmas morning nearing its conclusion, Matt and I pile Billy's still unopened presents on my Grandmother Edwards' piano bench in the living room. It takes him the rest of school vacation to open his presents.

Every Christmas Billy watches *The Snowman* without fail while we eat brunch in the dining room. In Billy's still beloved video of Raymond Brigg's book, *The Snowman*, the little boy and the snowman embark on an aerial voyage in the middle of the night. They bear witness to sights the little boy's family will never see or know, traveling the world holding "tightly each other's hand." Along the way, they make pit stops to feast, play, joke, dance a jig, and marvel at all of nature's bounty. In the video depiction, neither the Snowman nor the boy speak. Their language is a landscape of visual and physical prose accompanied by a beautiful yet haunting musical score. Enraptured by their journey, Billy watches and listens. In the silent, dark night, the little boy and the snowman are "walking in the air" together but once the day breaks and the sun rises, the snowman melts away. For Matt and I, Christmas in Ohio is exhilarating and exhaustive—a precarious flight of faith.

Winter Run

Matt and I have just come back from an invigorating winter run. It is dusk as we join my Mom and Dad in the library. The library is a paneled room with built-in bookcases that line the walls. The books are the compendium of my parents' literary interests and moral passions. Cuddled up in scotch-plaid afghans they are watching a football game or the national evening news. I don't recall.

I sit down sideways on the upholstered, blue-and-green striped wingchair from my childhood. My legs are draped over the arm. Legs dangling, I am content. The winter run tingles my flushed skin. It feels good to sink into this chair in this room. I glance at the TV screen for a moment and ask casually, "Where's Billy?" The group consensus is that he had just gone upstairs.

I wander up the stairs to the third floor where the cousins are camped out for Christmas vacation. Two twin beds and an inflated double mattress are positioned in a row. Clothes, blankets, and toys are strewn in every corner of this spacious room. It is the annual holiday mess. I do not see Billy. I quickly move down the stairs to the second floor and scan every bedroom and bathroom. Running down to the first floor, I announce at the entrance to the library that Billy is not upstairs. Dad stands up and reiterates that he is sure Billy is upstairs. He seems concerned but confident. No one stays seated. The message is a jolt. Mom, Dad, and Matt rush helter-skelter in every direction. No Billy. I run into the kitchen. The backdoor that leads to the backyard deck is cracked open. Through the kitchen windows I observe that the live Christmas tree, draped in white lights and mounting snowflakes, shimmers.

"He's outside," I shout.

My mother picks up their wall-mounted red dial tone phone and calls 911 while I put on someone's boots stacked in the back vestibule. It is cold and dark. There are light flurries and the streets are covered in a thin white blanket of ice and snow. Eerily silent, I comb the backyard. I see nothing. I hear nothing. I know that Billy is not in my family's yard. At the end of the driveway, I stop and look both ways. I'm not sure which way to go. I just start running in the middle of the street. The boots do not fit. They are too big. I grip my feet for traction. My voice echoes in the black sky. My eyes strain to identify Billy on the street, Billy on the sidewalk, Billy in a yard. Anywhere.

Billy has no shoes on. He is in his red-and-white striped cotton pajamas. I am aware of the lapse of time. I cannot control the effect of time or frostbite. My senses are in overdrive. My eyes strain to penetrate the black night. My voice howls. But the only noise that blares back into my ears is the sound of the oversized boots crunching in the snow. "Billy!" I wail. But even if Billy responds to my outpour, he is forever silent. Billy cannot say, "I'm here, Mom." I cannot bear this mental snapshot of Billy's vulnerability. My body and my brain disconnect. I am outside my body. My body runs and searches for Billy. And my mind reels every morbid outcome. Festive lights adorn the neighborhood. It is two days before Christmas. Family gatherings and parties are happening. All I can hope is that Billy has not been hit by a car, abducted, or suffering alone.

The police cruiser is parked in front of my parents' house. The red light blinks. Matt says to me that the officer found him blocks away in someone's front yard. Silent, still, and terrified. I open the car door and Billy leaps into my arms. His blonde hair is still slightly wet from taking a bath.

Repercussions

B illy is safe. But Ben is not. Ben is ten years old. My mom tells me that Ben is upset. I move to find my son. As I push open the paneled library door that leads to the bathroom, I see my ten-year-old Ben in the bathtub. His body submerged, only his tearful face is visible. That's enough.

Anguished, Ben asks me if we found his brother Billy. The seams of my face want to burst and overflow with tears but I cannot unravel in front of Ben. I reassure Ben that Billy is okay. Everything is fine. Ben loves fairy tales where evil and goodness are locked in harrowing battles. This wasn't a fairy tale with heroic deeds and a swashbuckler ending. Ben and I know that fairy tales are fictional. Almost losing Billy was not.

I never slept that night. I listened for every door cracking, every footstep, every human and inhuman stirring. Nothing happened. Everything changed that night. Every night I double-check that the doors are locked. My wrist sports a house key on a coiled loop. Doors are locked from the inside to the outside world. My brother-in-law made a joke about the new regime. He referenced the Sean Penn movie, *Dead Man Walking*. Unlocking the bolted door to accompany Billy to the barn for a jump on the trampoline, he announced in an official voice: "Dead man walking." Dark humor. Relief.

The next day is Sunday morning. My neck is locked. I cannot turn my head either way to see without pain. My visual periphery is exhausted. It is as if in the search for Billy, I too froze. My body amplifies my compressed fears. Somehow my mother found and scheduled a masseuse appointment for that Sunday afternoon. Rubbing out the knots is hard work. Even this woman's healing hands and heart can only alleviate the surface impact.

The next evening at the approximate same time he was lost and found in the front yard of a stranger's home, I find Billy weeping. It is not coincidental. Huddled on the floor in his red-striped pajamas lying on the dining room floor in front of the 1940s style metal covered heater, Billy relives those moments of utter isolation. His tears run hard down his face. So do mine. The live Christmas tree on the deck reflects the lights' movement through the windows. The crystal chandelier draped in decorative holly is centered over an oval mahogany table set with linen, napkins, flowers, candles, and crystal goblets. Celebration is imminent.

Back home after the holidays, we resume our family work schedule. Matt goes to the office and the boys return to school. That week I attend a meeting at a committee member's home to work on ways to educate the community about children with special needs. We gather at the kitchen table with steaming coffee, pastries, and friends with a mutual agenda. In the past, our camaraderie was a source of comfort. Today, it doesn't help. Like in the Church of Christ that I grew up in, I need to confess my sins, lay out my emotional burden and be welcomed back into the fold. I blurt out that I'd almost lost Billy. Shades of alarm and concern pass across their faces. And then, nothing. Losing a child is the unthinkable. The conversation concludes that Billy is safe and that is all that matters. I am not consoled. I want to weep and thrash and declare that Billy was never going to be safe. Like Billy, I understand what it must be like not to be heard. This emotional islet is barren.

Santa Fe

A couple days before our family trip to Santa Fe, I take Billy to the pediatrician for his last round of vaccinations. Billy is seven years old. We are a bit behind schedule in terms of his childhood shots and the doctor is eager to make sure Billy completes the MMR regimen. I'm slightly anxious. There are some reports on various fronts suggesting that the preservative thimerosal may be unsafe for individuals on the autism spectrum. I raise my concerns with Billy's doctors. He reassures me that I needn't worry and that this is a responsible course of action in terms of protecting Billy from health problems. I defer to the expert and Billy is administered the shots.

Two days later, my parents and my family are vacationing in Santa Fe. Matt and I have rented a house so that we are all together. It is dinnertime and I call Billy and Ben to the table. Ben is hungry and digs in. Billy does not eat. I encourage Billy to get started. Hamburgers and French fries are a guaranteed culinary winner. Billy makes no gesture to move his hands toward his silverware or food. He is stuck. I hand him his hamburger. Billy can hardly hold the hamburger in his hands. There is no momentum. There is no dexterity. It's as if he's forgotten how to eat. With painstaking slowness and my guiding narrative at each step of the eating process, Billy completes his meal. This is not normal. By reputation, Billy is a fast eater. Every mealtime until now, I would have pointed to the plate indicating to Billy to put his fork or spoon down in between bites. Billy is Speedy Gonzales.

I've seen this extreme delay of motor planning once before. At the age of five, Billy was up every night. He would go to sleep promptly but then at 2:00 in the morning he would wake up and stay up until dawn. Matt and I referred to Billy as our "party boy." Jumping on the bed, running up and down the hall, checking out the contents of the refrigerator, Billy was a happy reveler. Then he would crash and our alarm clock would ring. With the doctor's approval, we gave Billy Tylenol PM. We needed sleep. Several weeks later, Billy exhibited an "acute motor planning problem." We rushed Billy to the emergency room. The doctor in charge handed Billy a tissue box and asked him to take the tissue out of the box. Billy understood the request but his ability to formulate the action was impaired. The doctor concluded that Billy's symptoms were an allergic reaction to the antihistamine. Billy's motor planning ability would return in time.

Our Santa Fe trip is riddled with questions. The only new variable introduced to Billy is the third round of the MMR vaccinations. It is a month before Billy's motor planning is normal again. Highly sensitive, Billy suffers from a litany of environmental allergies. He is allergic to penicillin and a host of other antibiotics. Rashes that look like red spider webs travel his limbs. His cheeks are always too blotched. Billy's medical record alone should have deemed that he was at risk. No one considered the possibility. Evidence of harm happened in Santa Fe.

Frozen Like a
Deer in Headlights

Billy is growing. He is in elementary school and I can no longer help him clean his back molars without standing on top of the toilet seat. Perched on the toilet seat provides an aerial perspective from which to see and reach his teeth. Playfully Billy turns his toothy grin toward me as I angle the toothbrush and entreat him to keep his mouth wide open. It's a routine we've done together for years. It feels ordinary. Seamless. Finished, I hand Billy his Oral B electric toothbrush and he places it back in the charger. Just as Billy turns toward me, I slip and tumble bottom first down the white porcelain toilet. It was the white socks that caused me to slide off the top of the toilet seat and land hard on the bathroom tile floor. My tailbone is glued against the outer edge of the toilet base. Sprawled on the floor in a bathrobe-entwined heap, I holler. Invectives may have passed my lips. Shrieking, however, realigns my senses and dulls the immediate pain flash. My vision refocuses on what is in front of me. Billy. Frozen, like a deer in the headlights, he hears and sees my pain. His facial muscles are taut. His brow is raised, lines etched on his forehead. His eyes are riveted on my compromised condition. He does not move. Suspended by alarm, he has no idea what to do. Billy and I stare at each other. Billy is not unaware. Billy is not expressionless. Billy is not disinterested. He is distraught. Clad in my nightgown and robe with a tailbone that throbs, Billy stands attentive with me in our corridor-tight bathroom. Neither one of us knows what is next. We just know that we are together.

Marching Ants

When there is no visible evidence, research data, or historical precedent, it is easy to dismiss. No one believes that Billy will be able to independently access multiple pages on a computer voice output communication system. It's a wait-and-see game. Meanwhile I insist that they include Billy in circle time even if it means the teacher must model his script for him.

For six months, Billy has taken his voice output computer, also known as "Dynavox," to join his class of five peers at circle time. Every day, Billy sits in a Samsonite chair with a fold-out table. His device is always on, but the general conclusion of the school team is that Billy doesn't use it. Or more emphatically, that Billy doesn't understand how to use the device. Every day I battle the prevailing tide of public sentiment and educational practices. I implore his teachers to model the specific page content and the navigational paths to other pages. My point is practical. Billy will never be a fluid communicator without adult guidance and encouragement. I know that Billy will use this device. It is not mother's intuition. It is a faith grounded in hard work, sweat, tears, and a culmination of microscopic breakthroughs. It is morning circle time and once again Billy's friend Arthur requests with great hoopla the song about the marching ants. That's fine. The problem is that Billy has heard it every single day of the calendar school year.

And then it happens. Billy says, "I don't like this." Maybe that morning, Billy had heard it one too many times. It's hard to say. But in that circle-time moment when the teacher was placing the "Marching Ants" song title on the board, Billy navigated away from his official "Circle Time" screen, went to another page, and without fanfare pressed the button. In a male computerized voice, Billy stated, "I don't like this." For the record, Billy stated the terms of his disagreement with the song selection and proceeded to navigate flawlessly back to the original page. Billy stared straight ahead as if no one had heard what he had just communicated. The teacher's jaw dropped and the scales fell from her wide-open eyes. That afternoon the teacher relayed the "astonishing" story. I heard him loud and clear. The teacher heard him loud and clear. It is a game changer. Billy is a nonverbal communicator.

Mustard Seed

Billy's educational program is year round. In the summer session, however, most of the head teachers and staff are on vacation. Billy's summer school teachers, however, are not up to speed. The transition is bumpy. With little time to review much less master each of the students' educational goals as stipulated in the Individual Educational Plan, or IEP, summer school is ad hoc in terms of substantive curriculum. Summer, however, is always a fruitful period in terms of Billy's readiness to learn. I scramble and privately hire a tutor for Billy. Without a committed communication partner, Billy would have no interactions. It would be abysmal.

Even though he is a visual learner who delights in colors, Billy has never been exposed to painting. His teacher and I decide to introduce Billy to the art world. I purchase an easel, acrylic paints, paper, and paint brushes. On paper we label in different areas the names of colors. I want Billy to imagine all the combination of colors at his disposal. Billy loves the rich palette. Reading the words, he selects a color and paints with a Jackson Pollack intensity. I've planted a mustard seed.

Part Three:
Middle-High School Years

Billy has always been incredibly physical. He is strong, he is coura- geous, and as he enters his teenage years, he is learning to become an independent communicator. There are, however, warning signs that go unheeded. His physical health begins to deteriorate, and his behavior becomes erratic. We consult with pediatricians and educators, but none of them are able to help Billy. We must look elsewhere for answers.

Superman Grows Up

Ben is in ninth grade. His nightly karaoke sessions with Billy are now brief. Now Ben has serious homework. Sitting at his desk in his bedroom, which is directly above Billy's rocking tire swing, Ben's eyes glaze over as he struggles to focus on his physics problem. Billy, however, has not left the music crypt. He soars in all directions to the latest pop and funk. Meanwhile Ben stares into space mesmerized by the vibrations and squeaking sounds of metal cable being pushed to its maximum capacity. His desk and everything on it shakes. Nightly, Ben experiences the earthquake ripples from Billy's superman frolic. Matt and I agree; Superman Billy is busting out. It's time to build a barn.

Celebrity Sighting

The three eight year old boys crane their necks to get a good look. Billy, who is in line with Matt at McDonalds, turns around to identify the source of the commotion. As if the paparazzi have sighted a celebrity, one of the boys turns to his mother and says, "That's Billy!"

At sixteen, Billy saunters into the gym taking no notice of the group of elementary aged kids who are slightly intimidated by his muscular girth and "take no prisoners" attitude. He's neither aloof nor oblivious. Billy is in the zone. Heading toward the trampoline, he effortlessly hoists himself on to the taut surface. Concentration is the game. The sky is his limit as Billy spirals his body like a rocket into space. At the apex of the ceiling, he extends his legs, sits in the air and turns his body 180 degrees. Floating down to the ground, he ascends again. Billy's flights of pikes, tucks, turns, and straddles are a dazzling display of body strength, control, and timing.

Billy is not fazed. As a child, the trampoline harbored much greater risks. Using the safety belt that was designed as a harness for little tikes, Patrick turned it into a loop swing. The objective was for Billy to jump feet first through the narrow opening and then without hesitation repeat the harrowing maneuver. With each successive rotation, Patrick increased the height of the loop until it hovered at heights that made me close my eyes in fear.

The next station is the pommel horse. Checking to see that his coach Patrick is in position to spot him, Billy is ready. As his strides gain momentum, he springs into continuous motion off the board. With his hands placed on the horse he transfers his body into a handstand that instantaneously pitches forward to a dismount.

Billy always ends his gymnastics workout with the rings. Holding the rings in his hand, Billy swings off the platform. Patrick slows down his velocity to a still point. On cue, Billy curls his body over and up into a reverse handstand. Arms are straight. Legs are straight. Not one piece of the apparatus moves. Billy forms one line of physical dexterity. For Billy, these feats are acts of sheer joy. Upside down, Billy looks at me grinning from ear to ear.

No wonder he is a celebrity.

Voice Colors
Project – 2005

It is the last week of school and the team is packing up the classroom. Half-packed cardboard boxes litter the worn tile floor. The staff is preparing for the summer recess. Entering the classroom to pick Billy up from school, I hear his high-pitched sounds of disapproval. Visually distressed, Billy tries multiple times to communicate his point of view. In a sweeping motion, Billy points to the suspect boxes. He retrieves his belongings that have been packed away, and puts them back on his desk. Acting as a physical barricade, he positions his body between the boxes and his teacher. No one listens or responds to his clear and earnest inquiries. Billy's repeated outcries will not disrupt their agenda.

Reading my agitated expression, the teacher quickly informs me that Billy isn't having a good day. No one has informed him that the school season is finished in two days. No explanation is given to Billy. Rarely are explanations given. The teacher suggests that I take home Billy's books. I hear Billy grind his teeth and I tell her, "not today".

Matt and I are at an impasse with the school staff. School personnel think that Billy's rudimentary hand signals, vocalizations, and body language suffice in getting his needs met. They are resistant to using Mayer Johnson's Boardmaker with Speaking Dynamically Pro Software as Billy's primary mode of communication. The teachers contend that I should accept and respect Billy as he is. I counter that the school is the educational laboratory to teach and support Billy in his communication endeavors. Most of the world will never interpret or understand Billy's vocalizations and body language as communication. I remind the staff that Billy's voice output system is universally understood and will enable him to have more communication opportunities. My arguments fall on deaf ears. Unless I provide irrefutable data, I'll never be able to change their prevailing mindset.

The bar for excellence is reset. I implement an intensive, communication-based summer homeschool program. I consult with speech and language and ABA therapists to design a curriculum that will systematically break down and impart all the skills involved in becoming an independent communicator. We create visual symbols paired with text, which guide Billy through every element involved in a communication exchange. For example, if Billy wants take a break from home school, he can't just leave unannounced. He must ask for a break. Pointing out the window is no longer an acceptable way to ask when Dad is coming home. He now has to use his device to ask the question. Our goal is to shape his behaviors into meaningful and universally understood social exchanges.

All summer Billy listens intently and learns. Every day he displays humor, patience, and focus even when he is unsure of what we are asking him to do. Billy's teachers Holly and Liz treat Billy as a communicator, and he begins to respond in turn. For the first time, he realizes the benefits of social relationships based on mutual trust and respect. There is a seismic shift in how Billy understands his role as a communicator. By the end of the summer, Billy grasps the concept that the device is his language system. Billy has become fluent in his own voice.

All summer, we film Billy's progress as a way to highlight our teaching strategies, and their efficacy. The hours of raw footage eventually became the documentary film, *Voice Colors - Billy's Story*. I had no idea that the results of this summer project would become a critical lifeline for Billy in just a few short years.

Cape Cod Push Backs

Billy is sixteen years old. Adolescence is a tough period. All autism experts warned us about how difficult the transition to adulthood would be. The statements, however, lacked any specific information. I had no idea what to expect. But I never expected that Billy would become physically aggressive. By temperament, Billy was never agitated. He was boisterous, active, and exuberant. Never vindictive, Billy was the little boy who wouldn't retaliate when other students in the classroom targeted him. I wanted him to learn to fight back; defend himself against bodily harm. The teacher reported that Billy made no automatic gestures to stand his ground. Lacking the killer instinct, he never displayed bouts of anger. Billy was not an aggressor. Billy needed a protector.

On that afternoon at Cape Cod, however, all bets are off. We are situated in our bedroom. Matt and I flank Billy. He stands between us forming a circle. Billy is demonstrably livid and we have no idea why. Defiant, his face flashes anger. There is a darkness that veils his eyes. Shirtless and in shorts, Billy is muscular, fit and pumping adrenaline. His breathing is hard and audible. His chest expands and heaves up and down. Arm muscles contracted, the trigger clicks and he lunges at us. Pillows and side tables fly. Body blows land. No one is innocent in this bedroom mayhem. Everyone is pumped. Pushing back, we demand that he stop. But that is not an option. Billy's mental and physical body is wired taut. At that moment in time he cannot will his retreat. Standing, his body sways side to side and up and down. An enraged Billy is threatening to himself and us. Unfiltered rage breeds vulnerability, and Matt and I feel vulnerable. Billy feels vulnerable. Exhaustion finally ensues and Billy's outbursts wane. I'm afraid, however, that tomorrow we will be back on the war front.

We make an emergency call to a psychopharmacologist to see if there is a medication that will calm his central nervous system. We administer the drug. Billy's central nervous system is not calm, it is suppressed. It is a compress that stops the bleeding. I'm not sure for how long.

A Routine Gone Amok

"Billy, it's time to get up." Billy is dead asleep. His eyeballs roll into his head as he hears my voice. He cannot focus. His eyelids act as shields to the light streaming in his bedroom. His movements drag. He has no idea what has happened. Fog envelops the day. Neither one of us knows what to do.

The bed sheets are drenched. The blankets are soggy. The smell is of heavy urine. I yank the bedding off and in separate trips lug it to the washer located down the hall in Billy's bathroom. It is 6:30 a.m. It is a weekday and in an hour, I will drive Billy to his school twenty-two miles away. Visibly upset, he recoils at the sight of his wet clothing and runs helter-skelter to the bathroom to discard his garments in a hamper. At sixteen years old, I try to assist Billy as he clamors for towels, new boxers and pajamas. I hand him wipes and point as he furiously removes the urine from his body. Billy is embarrassed and incensed. I want to give him his privacy, but I cannot. Billy needs my assistance. He also needs a modicum of privacy.

This is not easy for Billy. This is not easy for me.

I don't know why he wets the bed most nights.

Billy doesn't know why. This has never happened before. He has no history of bed-wetting. This is the information that I give the pediatrician. This is the information I give to the psychopharmacologist. There are no questions. There are no words of advice. There is no counsel. They are stuck in the mire of the diagnosis. Billy has severe autism. Billy is non-verbal. Further evaluation is not warranted.

Every morning we too are stuck in this narrow bathroom space repeating this humiliating routine.

Throwing Up

Billy's routines or rituals associated with a specific activity sometimes fade, re-emerge, or evolve. This pattern, however, is different. Unlike the others, it doesn't seem harmless. On a subliminal level, it is alarming. Matt and I don't know why Billy throws up with searing gut force at every restaurant meal. On Thursday nights, Billy the food connoisseur and Matt huddle over the device negotiating that weekend's social schedule. With inordinate care and deliberation, Billy presses the specific Speaking Dynamically Pro restaurant icon buttons on his Panasonic Toughbook computer. He is a passionate reviewer about his dining choices and often pauses and then, halting, presses the button, "I changed my mind." Lighthearted and playful, neither Matt nor I detect any visual cues that Billy is in trouble. All of Billy's communiqués express certitude and engaged excitement about the upcoming restaurant excursions. The lunch destination plans are set. On Saturday, Billy eats breakfast just fine and Matt and Billy go shopping and then to lunch. There are no antecedents. All warning signs malfunction.

Like us, I don't think Billy knows that his body is in turmoil. Yet, every weekend it happens. As soon as Billy finishes his meal he regurgitates every piece selected on the menu. It is as if in that instant his brain and body are disconnected, and a shadow crosses Billy's face. Caught off guard, Billy freezes. In that split moment, Matt whisks a dazed Billy to the men's restroom.

On Saturday evening, Matt recounts to me the bathroom rush and we brainstorm about how to avoid another public scene. Bags, napkins, and timing are all duly noted. We think our radar alert is code red. Dogged supervision and preparations are our tactical strategies. We want Billy to succeed. These outings are Billy's window to learning about the world. Being confined to a substantially separate classroom and home reinforces the idea that his life is static.

We adapt. We never probe why Billy is vomiting at restaurants because we think it's an autistic idiosyncrasy.

So every Saturday night, Matt shares with me how he took action and avoided a near miss. In each venue, Matt adapts skillfully to the rapidly changing circumstances. At Dunkin' Donuts, Matt is discreet. Careful not to agitate Billy, he holds under the table an emptied white Dunkin bag in preparation for what might happen. Sometimes the plan is useless. There is no exit. There is no time. In a last-ditch effort to shield other paying customers' eyes from the vomit spew, Matt piles linen table napkins over the scene.

Upset and distressed, Billy sobs. But we do not understand. Consumed with the immediate fallout, Matt and I do not analyze the growing data points in medical terms. Instead we focus on the mechanics. A naturally strong esophagus reflux, whole-food swallowing with breathtaking speed and phlegm-producing allergies are convincing theories as to why Billy vomits with such regularity.

It isn't limited to restaurants. At home, Billy sits down at the table for dinner and relishes every bite. Food is his fondest ally. Billy smiles, navigates to the food page, selects condiments, and asks by name for the ketchup. He is so fluent and adept at asserting his point of view. Then it happens. The look of haunted disbelief passes across his face. As soon as he finishes, his head is over the kitchen stainless steel sink.

Periodically I receive school notes that Billy vomited after lunch. The written reports state the facts but do not suggest a problem. At the end of the school day, I pick up a content and unfazed Billy.

The teachers are used to it. We are used to it. The teachers manage it. We manage it. Odd behavior patterns are inherent in autism.

Doctor Blind-Sided
Summer 2007

Billy is seventeen years old and we are at the pediatrician's office. We are there for an annual physical but my focus is on Billy's weekly bouts of catapult-vomiting his meals. It's a legitimate concern. It warrants a deliberate answer. Out in the hallway, Billy steps on the scale. I am told that his weight is still in the acceptable range even though he has lost seven pounds year-to-date. This statement seems overly confident. I'm uneasy. Billy does gymnastics, works out, and eats plenty. Why would an adolescent lose weight? We re-enter the examination room. The interior room is cramped and stuffy. Billy stands, moves, and sits in a continuous and blurred rotation. The doctor walks in, greets Billy with a smile and sits down at his desk with a mound of paperwork on Billy's elusive medical history. In these tight quarters, I stand facing the doctor to give Billy more space to pace, jump, cope, and wait. With his hand on his furrowed brow, the doctor sifts through the voluminous accounts of rashes, ear infections, and reactions to antibiotics. I suggest to the doctor, who smiles knowingly at Billy's quirks, that perhaps Billy has acid reflux and inquire whether giving him Tums might be helpful.

"It sure won't hurt him," the doctor says.

I reiterate that Billy's weekly food expulsions are violent and that this pattern is now in its sixth month. Why would an active young man who eats well lose weight? The doctor reassures me that physically Billy is in the normal range. His bulimic episodes are just Billy. There is nothing to worry about. Billy is stuck, but that's the norm.

Crotched Mountain Afternoon Nap, Fall 2007

It is September and Billy's vomiting episodes evaporate. Matt and I are so busy working and taking care of Billy that it almost seems like another blip in the scheme of Billy's ordeals. Perhaps the doctor's remedy of Tums is enough. This autumn signifies a new school year and I am eager to expand Billy's social horizons. In the spring, David, Billy's speech-and-language therapist, mentioned in passing that Crotched Mountain School was just about to complete a new recycling facility that would include students in its daily operations. I latch on to the idea that Billy should learn about work in this educational environment dedicated to working with students who experience a diverse range of physical and cognitive challenges.

Two days a week Billy, Billy's tutor Holly and I travel to New Hampshire to the Crotched Mountain School. The new recycling facility is an innovative initiative in that it addresses the refuse of the educational and medical complexes. The new plant is also designed as an educational forum for students with physical and developmental challenges. In a fully operating plant, students work, learn, and hone their skills in a real-time setting. The men who operate the facility are also there to assist and support student endeavors. An educational internship allows Holly and me to fine-tune Billy's visual work systems and introduce Billy to the world of work. Billy catches on quickly to all the work requirements and steps involved in any one task. He wears the protective gloves, places each steel can under the lid-remover attached to the beat-up table, and cranks off the metal lid. With the Top-40 radio channel as accompaniment, Billy pitches the steel tops into the assigned container and then places the can on the floor and fearlessly smashes it with his work boot. The "accordion" can is then tossed into an enormous cardboard retainer. At every location and with minimal introductory guidance, Billy completes every step independently, with focused precision. If he is not sure, Billy gets his device and asks Holly for help. I laugh and say to Holly that Billy is the poster child for autism success in the workforce. It is all so promising. At the end of the day, Billy walks into the work area and shakes hands with the guys. Holly and I are so proud of him that we are practically giddy every Monday and Wednesday on the drive home. We dare not speak. It seems almost too good to be true.

Down the winding mountain we stop at a drive-thru Dunkin' Donuts. Every imaginable doughnut and muffin has been programmed on Billy's device. With great self-satisfaction, Billy requests a pumpkin muffin, an autumn specialty. Sitting in the backseat with his seatbelt fastened, Billy beams. Still up to his old tricks, he holds up the muffin and impishly suggests that he ingest the wrapper. On cue, Holly and I whip our heads around and holler no. We fall for it. Billy smiles and delicately peels off the wrapper and puts it in the white plastic garbage bag strewn on the backseat floor. Billy gets the last laugh. Holly and I sip our coffees as we drive down the New Hampshire road toward home. The fall colors are mesmerizing. I glance back at Billy through the rear view mirror and comment to Holly that Billy is fast asleep. Seated, his head bobs up and down as he naps. I remark to Holly that I've never seen Billy sleep in the car. We both nod and I add that it must be the newness of his work routine that tires him out. Every week that fall, Billy nodded off in the car on the way home.

Blanket over His Head

Three days a week that fall into 2007, Billy enters the high-school classroom, smiles at no one, greets no one, and goes automatically to the designated "break area". He sits in a rocking chair and places a blanket over his head and body. Draped like a shroud, only his Nike sneakers show. He makes no sound but the silence is deafening. His body concealed under a blanket, Billy resides in the far corner of the classroom screened by a five-foot gray office divider. No adult sees him. No adult hears him. No adult appears concerned. No adult suggests or discusses the fact that his self-imposed exile underscores an unknown problem. Autism is the juggernaut. We all know that and so the questions are not raised. We are the ones who are mute. From the classroom-management perspective, the problem is that Billy refuses to accept the card indicating it is time to leave the break area and proceed with the work schedule. He answers. Billy crumples the card into a wad of contorted trash and casts it aside. He is not able to join in. He is not able to participate in the school agenda. Billy's point is definitive. Listening to Billy, however, is not part of the school agenda.

I stand speechless in the middle of the classroom. The vacuum of no questions and no answers alters my equilibrium. I sense the teachers' hardening justifications, mounting impatience, and battle fatigue. But the other reality is that Billy is alone because he cannot participate and the only way to convey his pain is self-imposed exile. My child buries himself in the "break" vault and I'm not sure he should leave. I'm not sure I should leave the classroom. I walk out to the school parking lot and wait in the car. Then I sneak back in the hallway to make sure I don't hear Billy crying. I quickly drive down the road and pick up a coffee. I return, turn off the ignition, and wait. But not for long. I think Billy needs to go home.

No More Yoga

I tell the slightly annoyed secretary at the front desk that we reserved the school stage area. Halfheartedly, she retrieves the key as we follow her to the side door. She unlocks it and Billy's yoga teacher Hannah, Billy, and myself enter a 1950s-style auditorium. We are on the high-school stage because this is the only place Billy can practice yoga. The auditorium is dimly lit and cavernous. In contrast, the stage is cramped and the overhead lighting is starkly bright. We are overexposed. The yoga sequence on Billy visual list is a simple sun salutation. He is well versed in this routine and his movements are fluent and athletically charged. On this January winter day, that's what I thought was going to happen on this high-school stage.

But yoga is not practiced. The mat is down. Rubberized cut outs of hands and feet are placed on the mat to guide Billy on the evolution of his yoga poses. The yoga schedule outlining the order, name, and picture of each yoga pose is presented top to bottom with a corresponding "finished" column. After completion of each pose, Billy will put the visual and text combination on the finished side. We are prepared. I have incorporated every documented approach and created others to support and guide Billy so that he can be as independent as possible. At age 18, Billy wears a Lululemon yoga tee shirt that stretches yet fits tightly to his muscular body. All the apparel is situated. There was, however, no yoga practiced. On that winter day, salutations died. Greetings to all livings things went subterranean.

What I saw that day was a human being tormented by pain and fighting like hell to be engaged in his life no matter what.

Billy goes to the mat and does one sun salutation that includes a downward dog and cobra. And then he steps off the mat. His feet together and his body in perfect standing alignment, Billy opens up his hands and extends his arms back wide and without even a moment of pause, his hands strike his face in rapid succession. The insane cycle repeats. Billy steps deliberately on to his mat and resumes the pose. He then moves carefully the pose icon on his schedule to the finished side. Stepping off his yoga mat, Billy executes the new mantra of pain. I just want him return to the mat. But he can't stay on the mat. Billy tells me the truth. I am in denial. Billy and I had fought so hard for a place on the mat. I won't surrender. Neither will Billy.

Part Four: Crisis

When Billy was seventeen, his body began to fail. He could no longer endure the physical pain. The intensity of his pain coincided with self-harm; he hit his face repeatedly. A year later, he began to get seizures. His communication of pain was alarming, dangerous, and with no known source. Billy may have been suffering through pain all his life. We don't know, and probably never will. But what we were soon to encounter was that Billy's mind-numbing pain would forever change the course of his life and ours. Autism, as a systems disorder, has many dimensions and we would discover what that meant in terms of the human impact. The physical, emotional, and spiritual effects are raw and unrelenting.

Autism is Idiosyncratic, But Not Ominous

It is early December and I notice that Billy occasionally hits his face. It seems out of character. The episodes, however, are infrequent and fleeting. I am busy. It is the holiday season. Autism is complex. I attribute Billy's actions in the context of autism. I tell myself that it will fade away. Historical precedents are abundant. For six months, Billy would navigate the kitchen in perpendicular lines. It was time consuming but harmless. Any household item that was not in its proper place—or that did not appear to have one—would end up in the toilet regardless of size. Every night after using the bathroom, Billy would try to dump detergent on an oriental rug in the same exact spot. All of Billy's autism propensities were annoying and odd, but not ominous.

Panoramic, But No Details

As an eighteen year old, Billy's open-hand strikes to the sides of his face accelerate. It is no longer an occasional episode. His self-inflicted lacerations cover the sides of his face. The skin is burnt red and swollen. In the area of his cheekbones the skin is sheared off. Seeping wounds and glazed eyes, Billy is tortured. Every day and every hour, Billy expresses his pain. We are overwhelmed with concern for these mysterious medical issues and we have no idea what they entail. We assume that because Billy's focus is on his face that he might have dental-related pain. I make a dental appointment. Wisdom teeth issues are at the top of my list.

Billy stands in front of the panoramic X-ray machine. Exhausted from the mounting pain, he looks utterly forlorn. Listless, he doesn't even flinch when the machine rotates closely around his face and head. A dental exam and X-ray results reveal nothing. His teeth look fine. We need to find the source of his pain. The Billy I know is disappearing.

Emergency Room Standoff

The current American medical system treats and refers patients in a linear mode. This format benefits healthy individuals. If you are ill and need a conglomerate of consults, the present system stalls. Invaluable time in diagnosis is lost and patient care is compromised. Doctors understand this dilemma. A collaborative review of Billy's health issues requires that this medical predicament become our burden. The only way we will get a team of specialists to assess Billy's case is to go to the emergency room.

Several months prior, the interior wall of Billy's mouth got infected after his tooth punctured the skin. With a diagnosis of buccal cellulitis, or acute inflammation of the skin, Billy went on an unsuccessful antibiotic regimen. I inform Billy's pediatrician that he still manifests pain symptoms. We are puzzled and concerned that his pain symptoms persist. It is Friday morning and the weekend is approaching. We don't want to ignore Billy's stress and we don't want to end up in ER on the weekend. Staffing won't be optimal. Specialists will not be available. Saturday night in an urban hospital with an eighteen-year-old young man who has autism and undiagnosed pain is not advisable for anyone.

Since Billy cannot tell us the source of his massive discomfort, his primary doctor advises that the safest and prudent course of action is to go to the emergency room. This is a daunting proposition on a Friday afternoon in the middle of pending snowstorm. His doctor reassures us that she will send a detailed account of Billy's medical history and give the staff a heads up that Billy has autism and requires special consideration. I am not reassured.

It is the middle of January. The roads are slick and visibility is poor but we arrive intact at Boston Children's Hospital's emergency room. As we approach the front desk, Matt and Billy sit down on some chairs adjacent to the registration area. Billy is visibly upset and cries out in anguish. Using the device, Matt tries to quell Billy's mounting anxiety.

I announce to the ER receptionist that Billy Megargel is here. With the speed, agility, and intensity of a college linebacker, Billy jumps me from behind. I bend forward to shelter my head and neck as Matt scrambles forward to release Billy's tenacious grip on my body. We are in a domestic brawl for all to see. Billy's act of desperation, anger, and survival instinct converge in front of a receptionist who has her finger now poised on the emergency red button, and two male attendants whose chests and shoulders flex in preparation for a take down. A short-lived altercation is over. Resettled, Matt and Billy converse on the device about the schedule details that will lead him back home. That fact seems not to register with the ER team. Testosterone levels are pitched. Our domestic altercation is about to evolve into a full-fledged rage. Instinctively I know that the staff views Billy's act as aggression. Assault. They cannot imagine that his behavior is communication of unbridled pain. Restraint procedures, however, are not a viable solution. He will only be confused and terrified by such actions. The other reality is that Billy needs to walk into medical facilities of his own accord. The physical act of restraint combined with the fear induced will cut off Billy's access to medical services he needs. I know this instantly. And then it happens. My instincts are on high alert. My responses are automatic and swift. An ancestral lineage steeped in the vowed defense of love and family ushers forth in my being like a volcanic eruption.

With the woman's hand poised over the red emergency button and several male attendants approaching, I yell, "Stop!" Eyes lock, and I declare that I don't need their help. They back off because my maternal instincts, prehistoric in origin, give them pause. This crisis is over.

Now I Lay Me Down to Sleep

It is late when I hear him weeping. It is always in the midnight darkness that Billy weeps. Initiating sleep is always difficult for him. His central nervous system bellows unrestrained adrenaline. The solitude of night intensifies his fears.

During the light of day, he copes. There are distractions, routines, and human contact that buoy his spirits in the midst of unknown and unfathomable pain. But at night, Billy sits in his red-plaid chair and rocks until his body can no longer tolerate the misfiring in his brain that permeates his bodily organs.

There is no outlet. In the night space, I hear the pace of his running gait. It is frenzied. The doors are dead bolted. Billy's red-plaid chair faces directly the narrow hallway that leads past the kitchen, dining room, and living room. The hallway ends in a tight but drafty front vestibule. On the wall is a gold-veneer, art-deco mirror that swirls and swags at each corner. In front of the mirror is a black, oriental-patterned planter that holds a deep green plant with outreaching leaves. Billy must know every iota of detail in this narrow hallway as he traverses the length of this dead-end corridor.

His screams drift eerily in the air and infiltrate my semi-conscious state. We huddle, knowing that soon Matt will roll his body out of our bed, walk out of the bedroom and gently shut the door behind him. We are all awake. But it is Matt who finds the sofa cushions and positions them in front of Billy's bedroom door. Groping in the pitch black for a pillow and a blanket, Matt lies his body down and waits. Hours pass. Eventually Billy's body will succumb to sleep. But Matt does not return to bed. He remains on the floor outside of Billy's bedroom. It is uncomfortable. It is exhausting. It is a nightly state of delirium. Matt never complains. He comforts us. His body frames Billy's space and his melodic snores of slumber lull me to sleep. He will always lay his body down in the hallway. It is Matt's sacrificial prayer that for the few hours remaining, Billy and I will know calmness.

In Their Professional Opinion, There is Nothing More They Can Do

The blows that Billy inflicts on the sides of his face cause a slightly angled tooth to puncture the skin, leaving the area vulnerable to infection. The ear-nose-and-throat specialist concludes that Billy has buccal cellulitis in the interior of his cheek. His regimen of antibiotics is finished. Upon a follow-up visit, the doctor concludes that Billy's infection is no longer the principle source of his ongoing pain. Politely distant, competent and thorough, she communicates that Billy's problem is not in her realm of specialization. Billy sits in the examination chair, looks directly at her and then ravages his face repeatedly. Her expression suggests detached pity. The sound echoes in the small examination room. She kindly suggests that we see a neurologist. There is nothing more she can do.

Beyond Medical Specialties February 2008

The waiting area of Ladders Clinic accommodates individuals on the autism spectrum, ranging in age from babies to adults. This is not an ideal setting when one's pain, suffering, and autism are intertwined. Matt calls ahead to find out how crowded the room is. Given the green light, Billy, Matt and I wait to see Dr. Bauman. Billy sits in a far corner of a cramped waiting room shielded on one side by a wall with his coat draped over his swollen face. Periodically he removes the coat and with hands open in supplication, he strikes powerfully the sides of his face. As if covered in Job's ashes, Billy places his coat back over his head. He sees no light. Matt and I wince and bow our heads. We are here to see Dr. Bauman because no other medical assessments can account for why Billy ravages the sides of his face.

Dr. Bauman is a world-renowned neurologist and researcher in the field of autism. We bring Billy here because no other medical venue understands Billy's symptoms as physical in nature. With limited data points discovered, his behavior convinces the specialists that his sorrowful story is about a brain disorder. The diagnosis of autism precludes identifying any credible markers to warrant further scrutiny of his condition, so I'm not sure what we will accomplish in this meeting. That faint but familiar sense of isolation returns. Once again, 15 years later, I am emotionally back in the trenches, fending off cultural attitudes about my son's humanity.

Shell-shocked by my son's self-flagellation, we are called in to Dr. Bauman's office. Billy lies down on the examining table and drapes his coat over his head. His body motionless, Dr. Bauman enters the room, notes with concern Billy's supine position and then takes a seat at the table with Matt and me. She listens as we review Billy's complex and mysterious medical history. After our review, Dr. Bauman attempts to examine Billy but his listless body will not cooperate. Gruffly, Billy rejects all professional initiatives. Dr. Bauman walks briskly over to the phone and in motion says in no uncertain terms that Billy is very sick and needs attention now. Steely and determined, she simultaneously dials the phone and informs us that she needs to reach Dr. Buie, a pediatric gastrointestinal specialist and Ladders' colleague. In another breath, Dr. Bauman shifts her attention to Dr. Buie and explains that this young man's deteriorating health and alarming expressions of pain require a gastrointestinal investigation.

Witnessing that one phone call, that one act of collaboration outside her domain, that one act of humility, that one act of unconditional care—I am moved and inspired. It is unprecedented. Dr. Bauman unabashedly states that she does not know what is wrong with Billy. It does not, however, deter her from making a decision based upon years of observing individuals on the autism spectrum. There are no substantive data points. Dr. Bauman perceives Billy's aggressive behaviors as purposeful communication that should not be ignored and she is willing to take a calculated risk and refers us to a specialist outside of the field of neurology. This is a model of effective medical care in action. By being open to an explanation that lies outside her specialization, Dr. Bauman changes the medical momentum and the prognosis. With one phone call, Billy will no longer be treated solely as a young man with autism. He will be treated as a patient who deserves a diagnosis and ongoing medical attention. In that brief phone transaction, my faith in others' help is renewed. I will carry on.

Eyes

Touching someone's eyes is an act of intimacy. Billy yearns to touch my eyes. His movements are awkward yet steely and determined as his arms and hands reach out toward my eyes. As he approaches me with his stilted walk and his arms extended, his eyes reveal pools of longing and incredulity born out of incessant bodily pain.

Billy's touch is not gruff, but I instinctively shield my eyes from his reach. His fingers rest on my closed eyelids. I recoil. Even though his touch is light, there is still a pressure bearing down on my eyeballs. At that instant, I cannot see. I feel as if my privacy has been breached. Uncomfortable, I step away and try to steer Billy's attention elsewhere. Anywhere.

Billy is not deterred or upset by my turning away. Instead, Billy's efforts are persistent. Touching my eyes is his only way to send a message for help. He needs me to see what I cannot see. He needs my insights, not my blindness. Billy needs my unflinching sensitivity toward his plight. As his pain cycles, his pain rituals become the drumbeat of his life.

Pain rituals are not autism rituals. There is a marked difference. Autism rituals exude a robust commentary. Billy's rhythmic patterns that punctuate daily routines, new events, and sensory fluctuations are the periods, commas, and exclamation marks of his life. His past repertoire of rituals provided a unique continuity and order to his world.

The touching of eyes, morning, noon, and night is a communication, a message of pain, and a call for help.

Even Billy Does A Double Take
April 2008

There is a lull in the onslaught of pain. Not really. Billy's pain remains. But like a boxer, he's leaning heavily on the ropes. His eyelids heavy, Billy is exhausted. There is no fight left in him. His movements are mechanical. His lips are pursed. His facial expression is frozen. The Billy I know has departed. Now I have to fight for him and myself.

We need to get out of this house. Our house has become a medical ward. Sleepless nights and rounds of meds blur the distinction between night and day. Matt and I take shifts on round-the-clock call. Billy's suffering is infinite. We need perspective. We need another angle on the story. I call my parents in Ohio and tell them that it's time to go to North Carolina. Unlike previous family vacations, we cannot fly. Billy is not well enough. This is a road trip. A long, two-day haul. Our goal is to drive from Boston to Richmond. The northeast corridor is densely populated. Bumper-to-bumper traffic entering the major urban areas is expected. April school vacation and Passover converge and the traffic is even heavier as we drive along the Bronx Expressway that skirts Manhattan.

For the entire trip from Boston to the New York area, Billy is stony faced. He sits with his spine erect and stares through his black Ray Ban shades. Holly, his tutor and friend in this medical odyssey, sits next to Billy. As we enter the Bronx, Billy shifts his position. In the front passenger seat, I turn around. Turned toward the car window, Billy glides his glasses to the tip of his nose, cocks his head, and peers over his lenses.

Billy has never seen the Bronx. It is a wonderful sight to behold. He is genuinely interested in the urban, cement-laden landscape. Captivated by the domino effect of high rise after high rise, Billy's Ray Bans remain on the tip of his nose as his eyes move upward to take in the sights. For a few minutes, pain is not Billy's viewpoint. Who knew it would be the Bronx that got his attention?

We Are Moving Forward – April 2008

Billy, Holly, Matt and I are on the road headed toward Holden Beach, North Carolina. Holden Beach is the place where as a ten year old, I crouched effortlessly for hours over a shimmering bed of olive shells. I was in awe of the intricate herringbone pattern displayed in mounds of sand along the shoreline. Natural beauty. As a young girl, Holden Beach is where I twirled and leaped on sand and ocean. Oozing sand, fiddler crabs, and crashing waves mesmerized me. At Holden Beach I felt grounded.

On this trip, Holden Beach is once again our destination point. We are on a Virginia two-lane highway. Sheets of rain batter the car at all angles. Visibility is minimal. The windshield fogs. The air is warm but the wind and rain are blinding. I cannot see what's ahead of me. I cannot see what's behind me. I cannot see what's next to me. Traveling down this road is dangerous. The risks are unknown. Matt suggests that we pull over under the approaching bridge and wait for the storm to pass. Delay is an impossibility. I cannot wait any longer.

Gripping the steering wheel, I sit up and lean forward. I just need to focus. Holly and Billy sit in the back seat. No one makes a sound. There is too much fear. Holly takes Billy's hand and holds it tight. He squeezes her hand in turn. It's my call. I'm in the eye of the storm. My jaw is clenched and my throat tightens but my words are clear.

"We are moving forward."

No Spring Vacation for Billy

The family gathers at Holden Beach. It is a Carolina spring. The air is light, salty, and filled with fragrant blossoms. Every day Matt and I ride our bikes to the end of the barrier island and back. Whether we ride fast or meander, there is always a view of the ocean. The rhythmic sound of the ocean waves crashing, rolling, and receding over the sand is ever-present. The sea oats float gently in the dunes. In sync with the moon, high tide and low tide mark time. The ebb and flow of the ocean soothes me. It has always been a constant in my life.

The house we rent is on the ocean side. There are panoramic views of the inlet that divides the beach from the barrier island in the distance. Behind the house is the Intracoastal Waterway where boats move up and down the east coast. Our two-hour morning bike ride is a rejuvenating reprieve. As we enter the house and walk upstairs to the first floor, we see through the dining-room window Mom and Dad sitting in Carolina rocking chairs and reading out on the sundeck. An adjoining bedroom with open French glass doors abuts the main living room area. It is where Billy dwells. He's lying in the middle of the queen-sized bed in this sun-filled room. His moans are hardly audible. But his eyes are glassy and his pupils are dilated. I cannot see his blue-green irises. They are besieged by blackness. His head is propped up with pillows and the blankets are pulled up to his nose. There is a video on but it acts as a noise filter. There is no entertainment in this room. The sun streams in the windows. The ocean is footsteps away. The marshes teem with natural life. We are in an oasis. Yet we are not. Billy never runs to see the ocean. He is too ill. He never dives head first into the breaking waves. He is too ill. He never jumps fearlessly into the surf. He is too ill. Holden Beach is now a place of endless joy and overwhelming grief. I never thought that would happen.

There is no spring break for Billy.

The Burger King Question

Billy's pain does not subside that spring. The only time he experiences any relief is when lying down. The blankets are placed up to his chin with his head lifted up on large square pillows. His eyelids are heavy, burdened by the unrelenting pain. Billy's life as he knows it has ended. Ice skating, skiing, gymnastics, working out, jumping sky high on his trampoline and swinging rhythmically to the music with his knees just brushing the barn rafter lights are gone. Bedridden, Billy at age 18 follows a skeletal schedule that consists of lying down, eating, and going to the bathroom. Some days there is no known daily schedule. Time moves only when Billy emerges from his bedroom in search of liquids or the bathroom. His formal education is on perpetual hold. The realities of the adult world are now his learning field. Although Billy's pain threshold is high, the endless stress engulfs him like a vice grip snuffing out his youth.

With fear and trepidation, we tell him. We tell him the truth. We don't try to deceive him or pad the story or omit the news. The afternoon before the medical procedure, using his device, we face Billy's anguished expression and in his language we point and press in succession to each symbol and word on the device. We verbally articulate that he is in pain and he needs to go the hospital for a colonoscopy and then he can come home. Weakened and vulnerable, Billy cries out as tears well in his eyes.

Pulling a kitchen chair to the counter, Billy hovers over the device. Matt and I stand next to him and review over and over the details of the next day. Then we all wait in silence, then we grieve. We review the day's events. Then we wait with Billy. We wait in undetermined time. Past present and future time doesn't matter. We hear. We feel Billy's fear and we never leave him alone in the kitchen with his device until he signals that this discussion has ended. It is his choice to close down the computer.

The next morning we get in the car, armed with a bag that contains a sage-green, velour-fringed afghan and an extra device in case of technological malfunction. As we back out of the driveway, Billy, always a warrior, lets out his best rebel protest. His fist pounds the backseat car window. Defiance blazoned on his face, the car rocks as he imparts his final fuck you to this whole expedition. We arrive at Mass General and park in the decrepit and dark garage where nobody wants to be. Physically ill, depleted by the last 48 hours of swigging a bottle of magnesium citrate, swallowing multiple Dulcolax dosages, and running repeatedly in a panic from his bed or sofa to the bathroom, Billy's resolve of resistance weakens.

Matt and I escort Billy into the Wang entrance of the hospital. He allows us to take the lead. The entrance to Mass General looks much more menacing when imagined from Billy's perspective. Wheelchairs litter the sidewalk, a courtesy bus parks right in front. Bus drivers and security guards congregate in front of the revolving doors. Patients, relatives, and doctors scurry to their appointments.

It's like navigating harrowing pinpoint turns with no room for a mistake. At any point in this odyssey to the gastrointestinal department anything can happen. There, in Billy's distant sight, is the much-anticipated coffee stand with glass encasements filled with bagels, muffins, and every other sugar fix. We knew this was coming—our first known minefield. Billy starts to move us in that direction and as we lean into him and steer him back toward the elevator, we promise repeatedly the eternal nectar. "Yes, Billy, first see doctor, then bagel and blueberry muffins." Still holding our breath, we arrive. But there is one more detour. Distraught by the sight of the waiting room, the visual reminder of why he is here, Billy drops his device bag and raises his hands. In rapid-fire motion, Billy executes blows to the sides of his already red beaten skin. There is nothing silent about his suffering. It is palpable and clear. The large waiting room is filled with mostly adults. It's very quiet. As we enter the glass-enclosed room, Billy grumbles his protest. Quickly we find a series of chairs removed from others and I hasten up to the front desk to announce our already known and anticipated arrival.

Taking Billy to different medical facilities requires a reconnaissance team mission. Matt had scouted the route, talked to the front desk staff and prepped them for how and why our administrative check-in required flexibility. So as Billy and Matt are now reviewing on the device the blueberry muffin/bagel promise, I reiterate that we need a quiet and separate space to wait and, no, Billy will not wear an ID wrist band or the blue hospital Johnny that flaps open in the back. These are rules that just don't compute. These prep steps would have to be taught in a deliberate, systematic fashion in a non-threatening environment. But there is no time, desire, or patience reserve left to explain this information to the attending personnel. The hospital social codes are foreign and inexplicable to Billy. It is irrelevant. Billy is a very sick young man who needs treatment and care now.

In the background, I hear Billy's anxiety level rise and turn back to the receptionist. I smile tightly and tell her to let us know when we can use the pediatric waiting area. Ushered in by a kind and responsive receptionist, Billy, Matt, and I enter a room designed for small children. Random toys and chewed picture books are scattered on a bookcase. The room is the size of a walk-in closet. But for our family, it is a safe haven. We are freed from the stares, expressions of alarm, disapproval, and pity. We breathe easier and set about making Billy as comfortable as possible. I know that all he wants to do is lie down, shut his eyes and screen out this saga, so I rearrange the furniture to allow him to rest. Billy, still a muscular eighteen-year-old, curls up in the fetal position with his head dipping over the edge of the chair. I stuff our nylon parkas under his head. It is a cramped space in an inner room. The air is stale.

I cover him up with the throw we brought from home. Billy lies very still. Under immense pressure to follow the protocol and, in great physical pain and discomfort, Billy lets go—a suspended calmness. We wait. The procedure requires that you arrive two hours early. So any delay makes the time lag seem relentless as each hour ticks by. Looking through the narrow pane of glass in the door, I see the hustle and pauses that punctuate the medical day. Billy rests, and Matt and I look at each other in silence. We are in disbelief that a patient with autism would have to wait so long. Incredulous, we whisper to each other that Billy may not be able to do this today. Mentally we prepare ourselves for this distinct possibility. Periodically the nurse opens the door and checks in. I'm not sure why. Billy never moves from the fetal position.

Almost four hours later, it is our turn, we wake Billy and with his device we tell him that it is time to see the doctor. We gather our coats, blanket, and Billy's computer bag that holds his back-up device. Billy stands, his device hanging from his neck and his black Ray Bans screening his blue eyes from the harsh reality. Street clothes on, he walks independently through the door toward the operating room. As we enter the designated room, I note the body tension springing from every member of the medical team. All are in position, prepared for anything.

The doctor is on the far side of the gurney, the anesthesiologist and her assistant stand by all the needles and tubes. The nurse is at the foot of the gurney and in the far right corner is some fellow on a computer. Billy, Matt, and I stand in a threesome. We place our gear in any corner we find in this capacity-filled room.

In those first long seconds, everyone is unnerved, uncertain as to what will take place—except Billy. Ray Bans still fixed on his face, he sits on the edge of the gurney. Matt and I wait for Billy's cue. He stands, walks two steps over to the adjacent table, picks up his device and sits back down. He turns it on and the familiar Windows music indicates the opening. In the middle of this poised, ready-to-go, blue-Johnny crowd, he navigates to the daily communication page and presses the button "weekend choices". Billy deftly selects the "restaurants" button, which produces a pop-up display of all his preferred dining locations. He looks up at his dad and motions that he needs to talk to him. Matt moves next to Billy and says, "What is it buddy?" Billy pauses, looks again at his dad, and asks "Burger King?" Immediately Matt presses, "Yes" on Billy's device.

In that split second, I hear the silent collective sound of relief. No, Billy is not about to bolt, tantrum, resist, scream, or aggress because he is nonverbal and has autism. Nor is Billy scared or angry. No, Billy has a question and a way to ask it. Billy is hungry. Deprived of food and drink for the entire day, his request is reasonable. It is a legitimate concern. As I screen the reactions of the medical team, I intuit at once that witnessing Billy ask his question, get an answer, and then lie down and put him arm out for anesthesia is revelatory. Even as I then stand over my son's face and count softly to 100 as they administer the cocktail, though anxious and bone weary, I am joyful.

This is a historical turning point. Billy passed the final exam. Billy initiated and executed a social interaction under duress in a foreign environment. Not one administrator or educator would have advocated for or believed that Billy was capable of such independent and fluid self-advocacy. I stand in awe of Billy.

Once Billy is sedated, Matt and I walk just outside the waiting area. The room is framed by a large glass enclosure with a bench underneath. A full-scale plaque to the right of the bench lists all the doctors' names aligned with their respective and prestigious specialties. From our perch on the bench, I'm confident I will see the doctor come out once the colonoscopy is completed. Hungry, tired and our nerves both frayed and in overdrive, I tell Matt to get us all blueberry muffins, bagels and, yes, coffee. Peering incessantly into the waiting room where no one is allowed to eat or drink, we find our solace in popping in mouthfuls of the fat blueberry muffin hidden in a white bag while guzzling coffee. It feels like such a luxurious treat. I know Billy will feel the same way when he bites into his ketchup-dripping Burger King sandwich.

No Attachments Please

With no observed progress, Billy undergoes his third colonoscopy in May. He is nineteen years old.

Billy still exudes a natural machismo. He was born that way, although perhaps his raucous family also encouraged it. Frankly, it is a genetic gift. Billy at 19 walks with a strutting stride. Shoulders naturally placed on his back, he shifts his muscular chest and arms in a rhythmic "I'm cool" cadence. From years of gymnastic workouts, Billy's hands are calloused, weathered, and strong. Offering Billy a high five is no laughing matter. His high fives are rapid, stinging affirmations of his instinctive bravado and lust for life. Billy's handshake is rough and commands your attention. His voice is deep and strong, his roar can give any seasoned professional pause.

So even in the recovery room, when most individuals savor the drug-induced stupor as a welcome buffer zone from the medical realities, Billy prefers to wake up and survey the situation. No amount of sedation thwarts Billy's presence. In this particular recovery unit, the nurses do not heed my warning that when Billy opens his eyes he is in full-throttle mode.

Eyes wide open, Billy begins his infamous search-and-find mission. Any piece of tape or gauze, no matter how small, is "history". All plastics, wires, and tubes are found and removed. The nurse cannot move fast enough. Billy's radar for locating foreign materials is rapid, precise, and not to be questioned.

His body cleared of all suspect items, Billy senses that something just isn't right. Peering under his hospital blankets, Billy discovers that his shorts, shoes, and socks are missing. Leaping to a sitting position, he demands the apparel be returned immediately. Without a hitch, Billy dons his shorts, puts on his socks and shoes, and ties each shoe with his signature six knots. Black Ray Bans strategically positioned on his nose, he pulls the blanket over his head and lies back down on his side. Order has been established and all is well in Billy-land!

Now Billy is ready to rest. In an effort to move the process along, the nurse suggests that we offer Billy a drink. Ah, now the piece de resistance. The nurse gives Billy a can of Mott's apple juice and a straw. In a move never seen at Mass General Hospital's gastrointestinal recovery room, Billy demonstrates his signature act. Never coming up for air, Billy inhales the juice through the straw, crushes the can and then shakes it up and down. This is Billy's version of a "final call".

Billy's final call accomplished.

The Shade Malfunctions

It is late morning and Billy will not get out of bed. Flashes of anger ignite his face as he bellows and points emphatically to the shade. The shade has become the Maginot line. Billy will not leave his bed until the shade is fixed. Sick and gutsy is a tough combination to reason with. I am flustered. Household technicalities are not my strong suit. The red-and-white pinstripe shade that covers the width of two adjoining windows will not spring into a closed roll at the top of the window frame. With various degrees of pressure applied, I try to coax the shade to spring tightly. It won't budge and neither will Billy. On my tiptoes, I balance on the back edge of the red plaid chair situated in front of the two windows and release the shade off the brackets. I roll it tight and put it back up. The shade will not roll up completely. While I try all these maneuvers, Billy lies in bed and growls and motions to the shade. He is ticked off. But so am I. I call Matt at the office. The phone call serves as a hotline for my mounting frustration. He does not offer solutions. Holly, who is downstairs in home school, hears all the commotion and comes upstairs to assist. Billy hollers. I yell. And Holly whips off her headband and bandages the shade. Five black headbands later, the shade is up. The window is clear of the shade impediment. Billy gains a modicum of control. Let the sun shine in.

For Billy, Summer is a Sliver of Time

For Billy, summer is a sliver of time. Almost imperceptible. Pain remains. There is, however, a brief lull; almost like a time out. I cannot explain why it happened. For three weeks in July we experience a summer hiatus. The most memorable time took place at our summer house in Orleans. The sky is crystal blue, the temperature is warm, and the breeze refreshing. The neon-colored noodles float atop the pool surface. The Nerf football flies through the air. The radio is blasting summertime hits. Ben and his cousins Matt and Alex are hanging out. It is a dudes' scene. Horseplay and wisecracks rule. No one expects Billy to make an appearance. He hasn't been in the pool once this summer. Then the clip moment happens. Billy saunters down to the pool area. He walks around the shrubs that frame the pool and steps on to the boulder at the edge of the pool. With a chessie-cat grin, he leaps into the air and jumps feet first into the deep end. Like a jellyfish he swims underwater, skirting the bottom of the pool. Billy is nineteen and for that shining moment he is just one of the guys. For Billy, however, lightness dims quickly.

Autism and Hospital Protocols
A Difficult Match

Search-and-find missions are always wrought with unknown dangers. Billy's colonoscopy is complete and Dr. Buie tells us to follow the nurse and attendants as they maneuver Billy down the hall. We walk briskly to be next to our son's still body. In anticipation that Billy may grab and pull out the IV, his left arm is heavily bandaged like a cast. As we enter the pediatric intensive care unit, Matt and I are stopped immediately by a woman who identifies herself as the doctor in charge. In a polite but curt tone, she informs us that we must wait outside the intensive care unit while the medical team situates Billy in his new room. We now enter a new and uncharted territory: a new department with new personnel, new rules, and limited knowledge about autism or Billy. Understandably, the medical team views Billy as a patient. But this young man has autism and a communication system that demands translation. In those short precious seconds before the door electronically closes and separates us from Billy, Matt and I try to impress upon the doctor how extraneous noise, light, human movement, and the absence of a communication partner could sabotage any medical objective and that it would be prudent for us to escort Billy. The doctor, however, has no questions, only directives. The button is pushed by the attendant, the doors slide open and Billy is whisked away.

The medical staff overseeing our son's case informs us in no uncertain terms that we must follow their protocol regardless of the fallout. This is the policy in this department. But we are not the norm. In those few minutes, as we are barred from being with Billy, I am thinking that even if he semi-awakens, the staff's medical experience will not equip them with the knowledge of how to proceed. Instead an emergency will unfold as bewildered and "alone," Billy wills his free arm and hand to remove all foreign attachments, tape, and gauze from his body. Physical restraint and medication will preempt any effort to communicate because no one knows his language system. This is my nightmare.

As these thoughts race through my mind, the nurse arrives and accompanies Matt and me to Billy's room. My instincts are on high alert and a snapshot view of the room compels me to direct. As the autism conductor, I fire out orders. "Close the blinds." "Dim the lights." "Speak softly or not at all." Pediatric intensive care protocol and routine procedures are about to careen into the equally gridiron world of autism. Despite all the drugs, Billy fights to wake up and take charge of his body. They don't understand his larger-than-life tenacity. Our objective is to keep Billy calm so that he will lie still for hours as the pellet passes through his lower intestinal tract. Despite my instructions, the doctors adjust his bed, reconnect the IV and move back and forth through the flapping curtain. They act as Billy's wake-up call. No matter what strength, type or variation of sedative administered, adrenaline surges through Billy's body.

Billy knows. His senses are not dulled but sharpened by the noise, the lights, and the pressure of the mounds of tape on his arm and chest. This is not going as planned. With every passing hour, different doctors, different specialists peer in, concerned and perplexed by what they observe. Matt and the nurse stand on one side of the hospital bed and I stand across on the other side of Billy's bed. Our hands are placed on Billy's chest and arms. We are not there to comfort Billy. We are there to physically hold him down as every 20 seconds his upper body struggles to rise and break our tackle.

We are his silent tormentors. Intimidation by force is the real sedative. Alert, Billy resists this assault every second and minute for four hours. With almost supernatural concentration, Billy waits to make his move. If the nurse leaves to update the chart or turns around to answer the anesthesiologist's question, Billy surges forward. If I leave for a restroom break or if Matt relaxes momentarily his hand pressure hold on Billy's arm, Billy struggles to make a break. It is relentless. Into the third hour, my lower back aches and my feet are leaden; I just want to get the reading. This cannot fail. The cost is too high and we need answers. We need information.

But I am angry. Sedation was how we were supposed to avoid this emotional catastrophe. A concerned doctor starts to order another sedative to the existing cocktail and I yell out, "no more!" I will not subject Billy to any more attempts to lure him into twilight sedation. The damage is done.

In the fourth hour, they complete the readings. The mission is complete. No longer a hostage, Billy sits up and with speed and dexterity removes all the tape, pads, wires, and the needle from his vein. Blood pulsates out and Billy refuses the nurse's attempt to place a gauze pad on his vein. Billy's blood colors the white sheets and his t-shirt. Infuriated and betrayed, Billy looks at Matt and hits him on the head. Power, remorse, humiliation, and an incendiary rage blanket his face. Matt holds Billy back and gently says, "No". We feel obliged to reassure the nurse that all is well and Matt and I thank her for her exceptional help. She tells us to take our time. Billy can stay as long as he needs.

We are alone. It is dusk. The light softens outside the large, square glass window. Billy sits on a built-in alcove vinyl seat that almost spans the length of the wall. I give Billy a pillow and our green afghan and encourage him to rest. But he will not rest. Instead, he rails against what he doesn't understand. His wails are loud and deep. Matt and I silently ache. No one ever told him what would take place after the colonoscopy. We were assured that Billy would remain sedated and thus relaxed as the pellet passed through his lower intestine and the X-rays were taken. By all accounts, this medical process would be seamless. That was the plan. It didn't happen that way. Sitting on the bench, Billy faces the truth as he reviews the information on his device and evaluates the information he never received. Facing us but intently focused on his communication device, Billy replays his hospital experience over and over and over. He presses "hospital," "colonoscopy". He stops. He cries, he quivers, and he begins the dirge again. Matt and I stand in a hospital room next to a bed of blood-splattered tangled sheets, a grieving son and know we are blessed. As dusk becomes night, we cannot comprehend wholly what just took place for Billy, for us, and for our family's humanity.

Several hours pass and it is now evening. The doctors and nurses have gone home or are attending to other patients. We are alone. Billy stands up from the bench. We are all ready to go home. In a line of three, Billy, Matt, and I walk around the interior corridor of the pediatric intensive care unit. Billy stops at the men's room and we wait. With his communication device strapped around his neck, Billy is composed and resolute as he walks straight ahead toward the electronically controlled doors. Billy's physical bearing denotes a proud and fiercely independent spirit. But Billy is also emotionally courageous. He seeks no retribution for the sustained force enacted upon him in the intensive care pediatric unit. He seeks closure. As we exit, I turn my head, nod and smile briefly at the doctors who watch our dignified procession move out the sliding doors. Billy is a class act.

Thanksgiving 2008

Despite the spring colonoscopies, medical findings and the medications administered, Billy's pain remains chronic and acute. On the eve of this holiday of gratitude, Billy's pain pitches off the chart of any pain scale. Billy and I are on a collision course and Thanksgiving is tomorrow.

It is the eve of Thanksgiving in Boston. It is the eve of Billy's nineteenth birthday. My parents, husband, son Ben, and my brother Bill are dining at the Sel de la Terre in the city. I would gladly be with them but I am not. I cannot be there. I am somewhere I've never been. I am in my pajamas with the phone clutched in my hand, looking for the doctor's cell phone number in my red, worn, archaic personal telephone book. I don't file alphabetically and it is difficult to decipher my "scribble". Distressed by my lack of organization, I finally find the doctor's faded number on the inside cover. Holding the crumbled phone book under the lamp, I dial the number.

The doctor's phone rings and she picks up. Billy is bizarre. That's what I think. But I need to sound reasonable. Sane. Screams echo down the hall as Billy runs and runs. His threshold for pain is breached. I take another tactic. I inform the doctor that the situation is untenable. She believes me. She has known Billy and me for years. Perhaps she hears Billy's screams. Without hesitation, she calls the pharmacy and orders the Vicodin. Matt will pick it up on his way home from the restaurant.

I can't join my family at the restaurant tonight. I cannot be with anyone. I am not myself. I am transfixed by the sight and sounds of Billy's whole body hemorrhaging.

Billy and I are on the edge of unraveling. Hour after hour, Billy screams bloody murder and runs back and forth down the narrow hallway as if he can outrun his perpetrator. I don't come out of my bedroom. Natalie, Billy's devoted companion, is here tonight and she has the burden of witnessing Billy's tearful dissolution. This night no one can console, comfort, or care for Billy. No one can console, comfort or care for me. Dragging my pillow, I sit down on the sofa in the family room and turn on the TV. The TV does not provide the reliable bedtime

135

lull. Neither does the Smutty Nose IPA. It's just a backdrop for my fetal response to Billy's thrashing wails. The phone rings every 15 minutes. It is Matt. Amidst a backdrop of ambient music and people socializing, Matt whispers to me, letting me know that he wants to be with Billy and me. Matt pleads with me to let him cancel the dinner festivities and come home. I beg him to stay. There is nothing to come home to. Tears roll down my cheeks. Perhaps the family gathering during this time of gratitude cuts open the cracks in my steely resolve.

I never saw Billy Thanksgiving Day. The Vicodin dulled his pain and mercifully, he slept.

Past Thanksgivings were always celebrated with panache. Billy was born on Thanksgiving Day in 1989 and so the tradition of Thanksgiving and Billy's birthday began in unison. The dining-room table was covered in a soft-pink, damask-linen tablecloth. The dishes were an assorted collection of antique plates edged in gold. The finely-etched crystal wine goblets and champagne glasses encircled autumn's glow of rust, gold, and crimson roses placed in vases in the center of the mahogany table. The chandelier adorned with green, amber, and amethyst crystal drops created the elegant soft lighting. We dressed for the occasion and dined at the evening hour in grand style.

On this Thanksgiving, we dine at the pinewood, overtly stressed kitchen table. We want to be close to Billy. We want to invite him to the table. My father says a prayer. Grateful to be together, we eat and drink and pray that Billy knows we're celebrating Thanksgiving with him.

It is one of the best Thanksgivings ever. There but by the grace of God go I.

May the Circle be Unbroken

Billy's nineteenth birthday was not celebrated on Sunday, November 23. The day came and went. Unacknowledged. Frail and sick but laser aware, Billy spies the presents piled up in the family room off the kitchen and then, bent over, retreats back to his room. Neither rest nor sleep rejuvenates his body or his spirit. The pain is in a Vicodin-induced holding pattern. I see the dulled pain lurk in Billy's eyes, depleted of youthful energy and optimism. The Sunday after Thanksgiving, Billy periodically makes appearances in the kitchen searching for any sign of succor. Neither food nor family entices him. Dressed in his t-shirt and baggy pajamas, he always leaves empty-handed.

From his bedroom just down the hall from the kitchen, Billy hears the voices of his Granny and Grandpa. He hears their laughter. He hears their questions. He hears their concerns. But there are still no answers. Our family lives with this pall and struggles moment to moment to cast off its shroud. Celebrations are no longer organized in advance. There are no elaborate plans or errands in preparation for special occasions. Celebrations are simple and mysterious. That evening after dinner, Billy wanders into the kitchen. His beloved animated show from Raymond Briggs, *The Snowman*, is finished. Perhaps Billy thinks about the boy and the snowman's wondrous journey into the sky freed from all life's fetters. Free to dance, free to laugh, free to smile, and free to be together. Perhaps the haunting yet enticing musical score, "Walking in the Air," soothes Billy's assaulted senses. I don't know. I do know that Billy's birthday matters to him and to me. I ask Billy if he would like to open his presents. Billy walks over to the steps leading into the family room and sits down next to his birthday bounty. Surrounded by his grandparents, Matt and me, Billy wills his life into this joyous moment. Slowly and gingerly, Billy opens each present. I read the card and tell Billy who the present is from. Listening, Billy smiles faintly. We applaud. We applaud Billy.

Wails of Pain in the Night – Winter 2009

There are no autism resources that will provide treatment support for Billy. Even though he suffers daily, no hospital will accept him. There is no viable recourse. There is no Plan B. What we have is each other. Wails of pain in the night grip my body. Every night, in the darkness of his bedroom, Billy's expressed pain consumes the night air. It is hard to breathe. I am in this pressurized chamber and there is no exit. Billy also searches for an escape hatch from his tormentor. Running back and forth down the length of the hallway, roars of anguish pierce my eardrums. My neck muscles raise and stiffen. I am on high alert. At this moment, however, there is nothing I can do. Neither Billy nor I have any control over this nocturnal dirge. Sitting in his red plaid bedroom chair, Billy rocks furiously to extricate his self from his body. He cries out like a mother who has lost a child. The sound is deep, hollow, and eternal. I listen and mourn.

Drenched in sweat, Billy will not rest until his physical body is exhausted and the morning light nears. Lying in bed, my jaw is clenched. My spine levitates and the back of my body ascends off the mattress. Every muscle contracts. Every cell is adrenaline charged. Sleep eludes me. Isolation is our stark reality. Even if I tried to convey our nightly storms, no one would believe me. It's too gothic. There is no hospital or care facility that will tolerate Billy's expressions of pain. Nighttime is a wake that never ends.

Neck Pain

Billy's pain ravages not only his body but mine as well. The subtle tremors and the eye dilation remain constant. His pain is off the Richter scale. Red welts line the sides of my neck. The doctors have no answers. So we wait and witness Billy unhinge.

It is morning. It is time for breakfast. I brace myself. The ritual of breakfast with Billy has become a war zone. The kitchen no longer harbors communal gatherings centered on food, fun, and gratitude. Our kitchen is a chamber of suffering. Matt and I know that Billy is gravely ill. Matt and I know that his acts of aggression are a brutal, violent plea. Matt and I also know that Billy's actions convey a significant message. Billy's billboard reads in neon red. The text screams, "Do not forget me. Do not abandon me to eternal suffering. Do not act as if breakfast or any other mundane, domestic activity will assuage the physical and mental assault on my body." Billy's acts of war are righteous. Retaliation by Matt or I would be betrayal—a renunciation of his truth.

There is no green zone. And so Billy lunges at my neck. Though his nails are cut, he burrows his fingers into the sides of my neck. As I struggle to release his grip, the curved nail cuts into the sides and front of my neck. Immediately red welts emerge. Perhaps he thinks that my pain will cancel his out. Perhaps the repeated distraction masks his own despair. I try to stop him, but his furor is raw and his adrenaline courses wildly, resulting in a rapid-fire series of aggressive moves. Scrambling to protect my already torn skin, I clip a towel around my neck as a way to buffer my skin from any further duress.

I brace myself. I'm not sure whether Billy will understand that the towel around my neck signifies that it is off limits or whether the towel will ignite his need to unleash his pain, his anger, and his frustration even more.

My towel solution doesn't work. Billy is furious. I'm frightened. I'm losing and I don't want to retaliate. It will do no good. So I run. I run with the cordless phone down the narrow hall into the front bathroom. Billy chases me. I shut the door and lock it just in time. Pounding on the door, he demands that I let him in. I know his actions are a cry for help.

I can no longer help him. I am too vulnerable. I call Matt at the office and tell him that I have locked myself in the bathroom. I tell him to come home. Billy and I are in trouble. Billy pounds the door. I hear him pacing. I hear him writhe. But I cannot open the door. My beloved son and I stand separated, apart. Neither one of us knows what to do next. Holly hears the commotion and rushes upstairs from home school and tries to comfort Billy but to no avail. Billy wants Holly to open the door. The door is locked.

Matt arrives home quickly. Visibly upset by what has transpired, he leans into Billy's face and tells him that he has to stop. Matt's tone is sharp. His facial expression is unyielding. Billy backs down. His pain exhausts all his adrenaline reserves. I shed tears. Billy whimpers like a wounded animal. Matt's eyes dart back and forth between us.

I make a decision. No more barriers. No more towels wrapped around the neck. No more defensive postures. No more verbal orders. No more offensive maneuvers. I will stand in Billy's corner of the ring. If he bleeds, I will bleed. If he wails out in the middle of the day or night, I will listen. If he lashes out, I will be still. I will remain calm. I will be his mother. I will love him. The visual image I bequeath to Billy is a powerful communiqué. My nonviolent posture in the face of his anguish gives Billy pause. Raising his arm as if poised to do bodily harm, he halts. Billy cannot strike. I am his mother. In his agony, he remembers.

No One Ever Tells You What a Seizure Looks Like – February 2009

No one ever tells you what a seizure is or what a seizure looks like. I was in fifth grade when I witnessed my classmate having a seizure on the floor in front of the entire class. I remember how startling it was to see a human being shaking uncontrollably. As a ten-year-old, it appeared surreal, otherworldly. What bothered me the most, however, was the utter silence afterward. After Janice left the classroom, the teacher returned to the math lesson. There was no pause. There was no explanation. I never knew what happened to Janice. On some level, the seizure experience never occurred.

Forty years later, my nineteen-year-old Billy and I are in the bathroom for the morning grooming routine. His pain is omnipresent. The doctors have no answers. The doctors have few questions. Weeks before, I was in a meeting with a preeminent neurologist and two hospital residents studying in the same field. I had brought in a film of Billy. The film showed Billy moaning and crying. The film also panned in on Billy's obvious hand, arm, and shoulder tremors. I had asked the question multiple times before, but I asked it again. Could this be a type of seizure or could it be a precursor? The answers were vague or overly confident. Or resigned in that the data, without a patient's input, remains unknown. There is data. But there is no attempt to problem solve. Billy's medical details are not clear from a textbook perspective. From a medical perspective, it is a cold case.

Leaving the clinic that day, I thought that they didn't get it. Billy and I were in the trenches and those tremors were ominous.

On the following Friday, Billy proceeds with his daily grooming routine. His bathroom is not an ideal location to have a seizure. The

EVE E. MEGARGEL

room is narrow. The floor is tiled and hard. There is no room. There is no ability to maneuver.

When danger ensues, I wonder if the brain processes the incoming information at a slower speed and thus with surprising clairvoyance. Standing on the toilet side of the bathroom, Billy raises his left arm, turns his head left, and collapses gradually to the floor. I shield his head from a direct hit to the tiled floor. Sprawled on the floor with his head locked between the toilet and the bathtub, his eyes are shut.

In the emergency room, he receives the customary Ativan and after some observation and review of vital signs, he is released. No one receives a prescription for anticonvulsant medication with only one seizure. We are informed that likelihood of future seizures is not common. What transpired in the bathroom was an aberration.

No One Ever Tells You What a Seizure Looks Like – Part 2

It is Monday morning. It has been forty-eight hours since Billy was taken to the emergency room for a seizure. Billy sits at a half-crescent shaped desk. Holly, his home-school teacher, sits directly across from him. Billy's communication device is situated on the table between them. Holly has a piece of paper and a pen poised to record the schedule Billy will dictate through his "Toughbook". Schedule talk is one of the few routines Billy is able to accomplish consistently. Although the content of his schedule is sparse, it nevertheless provides Billy with a finite and reassuring structure for the day.

With NPR as my listening backdrop, I'm in my bathroom putting on my signature 523 Excess de Rouge lipstick. This is a routine that is also comforting. Still focused on my makeup ritual, I hear a faint but urgent call of my name. Still reeling from our Friday morning ambulance escort, I run down the hallway and descend the stairs to home school. Seated at the table, Billy is experiencing a grand mal seizure. It looks like a prisoner electrocution. Almost elevated from his chair, every fiber in Billy's young body twitches violently. As his chest bolts back and forth, Billy's head thrusts up and down as if it is disconnected from his neck. His legs seesaw in unison with his flailing arm motions. Holly stands behind Billy and I stand beside Billy. As I scan his face for some sign of mutual recognition, I yell his name over and over. I know no other recourse than to believe that he will release himself from these current surges. And then, in a quiet and measured but serious manner, Holly tells me that Billy's lips are turning blue. The contortion of his neck is cutting off his oxygen supply. She tells me that we must get him to the ground and on his side. I never saw what Holly observed in those precious seconds. I never saw Billy's blue lips.

Depakote Rush

Within three days of a small dosage of Depakote to control his seizures, Billy is resurrected. For forty-eight hours, Billy jumps on the trampoline like a rocket, turning his body in mid-air as he descends. Focused but kidding around, Billy is the man of the hour as he saunters in to the neurologist's office. No one understands his transfiguration. Two mealtimes later, Billy's bliss evaporates. A short-lived hiatus. A cruel joke. A wake-up call that Billy is still underground.

Questions are Guideposts

Ben is in London for his second semester junior year abroad. Despite the transatlantic distance, we are in close contact. Ben is lonely, but determined to find a social network of friends in his new foreign and urban environment.

I am lonely, too. Unlike Ben, I am private and protective. I want to shield Ben from our suffering. I don't want Ben's college experience to be overshadowed by Billy's spiraling medical crisis. I want to know Ben's stories. Caring for Billy who is so ill depletes my energy. Like Ben, I, too, am disconnected.

The social isolation is uncomfortable, awkward, and deepens my weariness. My connection with Ben, however, is clear and familiar. It is comforting. It is a wintry Sunday evening as we converse on the phone. Ben sits in his closet size bedroom in the dorm that is in walking distance of Big Ben and I sit in my unmade bed. Ben fills me in on the quirky British version of academic protocol and the lackluster social scene. He lives in a dorm where everyone's door is shut and locked. Half the occupants use their rooms as pit stops and live elsewhere. Ben adds how he must be a sleuth in ascertaining when someone might be in the common area. It is a far cry from the robust social life Ben enjoys at the University of Michigan.

In turn, I report to Ben the latest medical issues concerning his brother's health and update him on the current interpretations of what might be the source of Billy's pain. My report is factual. My intent is to keep Ben apprised of his brother's medical plight. For Ben's sake and mine, however, I do not stray from the facts. I don't want to burden Ben. Ben listens intently and interjects pointed questions about Billy as well as the medical strategies.

And then there is this silent pause across our transatlantic line.

Ben asks me a simple question. "Will you ever have anything good to say?"

My blankets are rumpled and my bed sheets are twisted from nights of unfulfilled sleep. But those facts do not matter. This exchange does. Although it is late, I instinctively sit up in my bed. My senses are charged by this engagement. It's been a long time since someone asked me about the whole of my life. I want to answer his question. I want to struggle with the gauntlet laid down in such an unpretentious and thoughtful manner. Immediately the word "hope" unveils. I am struck by the power of the word and how long it has been since I embraced its healing salve. I tell Ben that I want to live with hope and will work to envision it. It's not a guarantee. It's a promise. Ben listens. We are both silent and connected. I am thankful for Ben's astute candor.

Forty Stitches Later
May 2008

Three years later, I call Matt on the telephone and ask him about the details of the day when Billy put his arm through a glass window. This is what I recall:

> <u>Forty</u> stitches.
>
> In the house, the phone rings. Billy is swinging at the barn.
>
> Natalie called—don't be alarmed—Billy hit the glass. You better come.
>
> Billy is running around, screaming, and glass shards in his arm and on the floor.
>
> Bleeding profusely. I call 911, tell him to stay still—trying to stop the bleeding.
>
> I can't get close to Billy. Police arrive outside, and Billy is running, hitting, and screaming.
>
> Finally, Billy's adrenaline comes down. Natalie talks to cop, and gets what we need for ER.
>
> There are two big pieces in his arm. I pull out a three-inch shard.
>
> I wrap his arm in a t-shirt all covered in blood.
>
> The ambulance arrives, and Billy is—thank God—willing to get into the ambulance.
>
> ER doctor sees Billy. He says he should be in adult care. Blood is everywhere. I tell him we are not going anywhere. The EMT keeps wheeling Billy into the pediatric area.

Matt holds Billy down. There's a deep flap of skin, and the doctor can't do regular stitches. There's no time. He has to use the staple gun.

Fearing seizures due to stress and trauma, the nurses administer Billy a dosage of Lorazepam.

Seeing the metal staples horrifies everyone. Finally, they wrap his arm to cover the wounds.

Matt and Billy walk out to wait. Billy guzzles water. Matt observes a mother with young child with an ear infection staring at him. He smiles back at her.

It turns out the deepest cut was in the upper bicep, almost to the bone. Thankfully, the torso cuts are shallow, and no major veins were threatened.

Matt fears that Billy will pick at the staples. But it never happened.

Graduation

I'm in the lobby of a pub in a bucolic setting. It's graduation weekend at Kenyon College in Gambier, Ohio. I flew in from Boston to meet my family and celebrate the graduation of my nephew, Alex. The pub is classic. Dark wood walls and buckling wood floors give one the impression that much frolic as well as intimate conversations transpire here. A college pub, lively conversation and a beautiful May afternoon; it is the epitome of pre-graduation rituals. I excuse myself from the round table to make a call home to check in. I think the call is perfunctory. Matt is there with Billy. Natalie is scheduled to help out. Every detail is covered. There is, however, no contingency plan for the extenuating circumstances that Matt reports. Over the phone, I hear Matt utter the words "window "glass, "arm, "blood, "ambulance," and "emergency room". I hear Matt calmly tell me that Billy has forty metal staples that extend from his upper bicep to his forearm and stitches in the areas where the glass sliced his flesh on his arm and torso in a zigzag pattern. I ask Matt how this could have happened. He tells me that Billy was at the barn with Natalie. He was swinging and listening to music. The last song ended. As he had done a million times before, Billy slowed the swing down, jumped off the swing, ran to the barn wall and placed his hands on the wall.

It is a routine. Routines are predictable. Routines signify order. Routines assure safety. Placing his hands in the precise space every time he finishes swinging is a time-tested cue that precedes turning the Sony CD player off. On this ordinary Friday afternoon, the barn routine is seamless. Except Billy doesn't place his hands on the hewn wall. The familiar routine goes helter skelter. First distortion, and then chaos. Billy catapults his left arm through the glass windowpane that is directly adjacent to the designated wall area. That's all Matt says to me. I cannot hear him speak. I just want to know if Billy is okay. Matt says yes.

And then I tell Matt that I'm glad he was there instead of me. It's a cocky and insensitive statement but it's the truth. We agree to talk later. We hang up. I am numb. I know I need to walk back to the table. I know my folks will ask me how Billy is. I know I will tell them what happened in a measured tone so as not to alarm them or spoil the festive mood. And then what do I do? I believe that Matt will take care of Billy. I'll reassure the party that Matt is in charge.

The graduation takes place the next morning. It is a cool, misty May morning. The lawns are lush and green. Parents, grandparents, sisters, brothers, aunts, uncles, and cousins stand at attention as the procession of graduates usher in and on to the stage. As each name is called with solemnity and excitement, the senior stands and walks across the stage to collect his college diploma and shake hands with all the academic dignitaries. As I watch each student file across the stage, I share their ebullient fervor. Possibilities are abundant.

And then my mind wanders to the barn and the backyard. Billy is screaming, thrashing, running, and circling the backyard as the glass shards pierce and hang off his skin and bone. The police officer arrives first. He steps back and lets Matt try to assist Billy. Blood is everywhere.

I applaud and smile as the students from this Kenyon class receive their diplomas. I scan the program looking for my nephew's name, Alex Caulfield. I don't want to miss this indelible moment in his young adult life. As a little boy, Alex would visit each summer and go to camp with his first cousin Ben or join us on family summer vacations. Billy adores Alex. In Billy's bedroom, there is a photo of little Billy sitting on his older cousin's lap. They are punch happy and giggling. The picture was taken at Holden Beach. Billy, Ben, and Alex are an imaginative trio. They never missed a moment of fun.

And then in my mind I see a blood-drenched Billy and Matt entering the ER by ambulance. It is a MASH scene and the lead doctor immediately announces that Billy should go to the adult unit. Matt says that he is under 21 and they are already in the pediatric section. Jamie, the EMS specialist, keeps rolling the gurney with Billy writhing in his own blood.

The commencement speaker is Anna Quindlen, a well-known author and journalist. Her daughter graduated from Kenyon the previous year. She is a thoughtful speaker. I lift my eyes upward to suggest my attentive state.

My actual attention is in the ER room. The decision is to use a staple gun because the skin is diced leaving a flap as well as irregular cuts. Stitches are too time intensive. So as people applaud the end of now honorary Dr. Quindlen's speech, I hear the abrasive snapping echo of the gun discharge each metal staple. The doctor is young and agile. But Billy is strong and quick. He is pinned down by two men as the gun shoots one staple at a time. For hours after this, Billy is exhausted. His energy sapped, Billy lies in the emergency-room bed. He never moves. The room is silent. Recovery is complex. Billy stirs. He has no intention of staying in this medical pod. Disoriented but determined, Billy walks slowly over to the refrigerator where the juices are kept. He remembers their exact location from a previous ER visit. He guzzles two cans and crushes them in his hand. Billy is ready to go home. Doused in blood, Billy and Matt depart. The next day, Billy is groggy, slow, and spent. He keenly observes his battered body punctured with metal. He never touches the staples. Billy doesn't want another horror show.

I can't recall exactly what we did after the graduation. We took some family pictures on the college green. I drove back to Cleveland with Mom and Dad.

Everyone was tired. An acute reaction to a higher dosage of Depakote impacts everyone.

After a serious dose reaction in May to the anti-seizure medication Depakote, Billy is prescribed Keppra and simultaneously weaned off Depakote. His system cannot tolerate the chemical imbalance.

Packing for Cape Cod Beach

I'm driving to the mall in search of a few summer accessories and it is the first time in over a year and a half that I've left my cell phone at home. I don't know why exactly. I'm not overly concerned. My errands will take no more than an hour. Turning the radio volume up, I override any lingering anxiety. I am excited about going to Cape Cod for the Fourth of July week. It has become our family tradition. Our son Ben, his college friends, my parents, brother, and fiancée will all be there to celebrate.

Family reunions at the beach bring back fond memories of summer vacations with my family in North Carolina. As a little girl growing up in Ohio, I would daydream about the smell, sound, and powerful beauty of the ocean. At bedtime, thoughts of dancing on the beach, shelling and eating dozens of southern-style hush puppies would happily lull me to sleep.

The ocean waits annually for our summer return. Billy is excited too about going to the Cape. The summer at the Cape is a welcome and joyous reprieve, especially this year.

Driving down our road on my return trip from the mall, my euphoria evaporates. I spot a fire engine parked in front of our house. I whip into the driveway and see a police car and ambulance. My heart racing, I run up the front-deck stairs. Holly, Billy's teacher, opens the kitchen door and says that Billy is okay. My kitchen is a sea of men bedecked in official uniforms and armed with medical bags and walkie-talkies.

"Where is Billy?" These are my first words to the crowd congregated in my kitchen. I turn my head to the left and behold my son. Peaked, bewildered, and lying limp on his side, resting on the family sofa, Billy looks so small, almost childlike. I fall down on my knees and caress his brow. Billy's forlorn eyes are open but introverted.

It is Friday afternoon and we are almost packed and ready to go to the Cape. Delay seems so unfair. I don't want to hear about any detours.

Billy and I are ready to go. In a respectful but resolute manner, however, the medic in charge informs me that Billy experienced a breakthrough seizure and needs to be transported by ambulance to the hospital. In transitioning from one seizure medication to another, there is a period of imbalance in terms of dosage. It is a risky process. If you go too slow, seizure is possible. If you go too fast in an effort to block a seizure episode, seizure is possible. Breakthrough is a step backwards. In the midst of packing his bag for the Cape, he yelled out, collapsed, stopped breathing momentarily, and went into full convulsion. This is a grand mal seizure.

I agree with the plan, but I tell the emergency medical team that I need to speak to my son, and could they wait outside. They file out and wait at their respective vehicles. The emergency lights blink, the sun shines, and I must tell Billy that once again all his hopes will be dashed by his malfunctioning body.

The message is mine alone to convey.

I walk over to Billy who now sits at the kitchen table and tell him that I need to talk to him. Using his device, I inform Billy that first he needs to go in the ambulance to the hospital and then we will go to Cape Cod Beach. Billy listens to my message, pauses, stands up and walks down the hall to his bedroom. Uncertain whether Billy will willingly go in the ambulance to the hospital, I follow his lead. The dresser drawer is open. Billy finishes the task at the exact moment in time when his body failed him. Methodically, he places the remaining number of socks in his travel bag. He returns to the kitchen and I follow in silence. Billy makes up his mind. He sits down on the kitchen chair and starts putting his Nike running shoes on. In reliable, ritual form, each sneaker is tied until there are no remnants of laces left to fold. Billy stands up, he situates his black Ray Bans firmly on his nose and strings the device strap around his neck. We open the kitchen door and hand in hand we walk down our red carpet to the ambulance's open doors. Star struck, our audience of emergency medics, police officers, and firemen gawk as unassisted and undeterred, Billy and I step up into the ambulance. Billy lies down on the gurney. It is so smooth.

Cape Cod Beach is just on the horizon.

Family Pictures

It is a monthly household task. Laura, our housekeeper, collects our framed family pictures from different rooms in the house. The silver-framed photos are placed on old towels spread out on the kitchen floor. The silver is dull or tarnished. Polish will bring out the sheen. Billy walks into the kitchen and immediately sees the array of family photos scattered on the white towels. Staring down at the pile of snapshots of family members smiling and jovial, Billy is disturbed by their displacement. His lips quiver and his eyes well up. His brow furrows and his facial features contort to the point that I cannot identify Billy. What I see moving across his countenance is sheer shock and disbelief. Billy looks at me as if I have desecrated hallowed ground by removing the family photos from their ancestral locations. Alarmed by his raw emotional reaction, I ask him if I should put them back. Billy bows his head and clicks his tongue to his upper palette. It is urgent. I start placing them back in their designated spots and inform Laura that we will clean the frames another time. The veil of darkness on Billy's face lifts and is replaced with a sigh of relief. He is not abandoned. Wherever Billy is in the house, he will find comfort in their constant presence. Permanent connections dwindle. But the visual remains.

Siren – July 2009

When I hear the sound of an ambulance siren, my spine tightens. My jaw stiffens. My eyes weigh heavy yet register alert. My neck strains as I track the direction of the fire engine, the ambulance, and the police car. On edge, I'm not sure of the emergency vehicles' destination. My cell phone gripped in my hand, I call home and the voice on the other end reports that Billy is fine.

I breathe relief. My body settles back down into its frame. I can now take a walk.

Taking a walk used to be an act of freedom. My legs would move briskly but my mind luxuriated in wonderment. No longer constricted by life's minutia, I imagined boundlessness. I was Harold creating with a purple crayon others' lives, other scenarios, other possibilities. The world brimmed with fresh ideas. As a child, I floated amidst a sea of daydreams. Dr. Seuss, Maurice Sendak's *Where The Wild Things Are,* and Grimms' Fairy Tales were my companions in my daily walks back and forth from elementary school. My mother recounts that on my first day of kindergarten, I insisted that I walk by myself to the new school. Walking alone in search of interesting observations has always enlivened my sense of curiosity.

As an adult, taking a walk orchestrates all my senses. The natural world envelops me. I listen to sounds that I rarely hear. The rhythmic beat of my shoes on the pavement and the swish of my clothes against my body set the cadence. Slowly, I become aware of other forgotten sounds. The croaking vibration of frogs, and grasshoppers, or water flowing in a creek bed over slippery rocks. Nature is the crescendo. I regale in the vibrant, ever-changing palette of the seasons. Hot air, moist air, frigid air, crisp air carry me forward in all my walks. My senses are restored and reclaimed.

I will never experience this walk again.

Broken Lines

We are at my parents' home in Cleveland Heights, Ohio. The renowned Cleveland Clinic is at University Circle, a short distance way. It is our final destination. The Boston doctors cannot determine all the sources of Billy's ongoing suffering. They have discovered, however, an array of maladies. GI issues and a seizure condition have been identified and addressed. But it is no salve for the level of pain and inertia that still plagues Billy. Billy's neurologist, Dr. Bauman, arranges for us to meet a specialist in mitochondrial disorders at the Cleveland Clinic. Mitochondrial dysfunction is the current hypothesis.

Although our mission is medical in nature, it is comforting to be with my family at my childhood home. The night before our medical appointment, we dine leisurely on the back deck. It is a warm July evening. The conversation is jovial. In the presence of my parents, we relax. For this evening, Billy is not under public scrutiny in our revolving medical sojourn and we are not absorbed by the minutia of medical data to consider. Billy is ill and Matt and I struggle daily to make sense of what is happening to Billy and what is happening to us. Here tonight, however, there are only well-wishers in our midst. The next afternoon my brother-in-law, Scott, leads the car caravan down to the Cleveland Clinic so that at least the trip is seamless. My spirits are buoyed by family support. Throughout our appointment Billy sits with Holly on the examination table. Blood tests, head measurements, and meticulous information gathering are accomplished. In the concluding moments, the doctor articulates his concern for Billy and us. I tell him that we need answers because this is not sustainable. The doctor readily agrees with the only conclusion cited. "Unsustainable". As we depart, it seems like a dead end.

The day after our appointment, Billy lies listless on the sofa upstairs in the TV room. Lying on his side, his face is mushed into the pillow. A blanket covers his torso. The TV is white noise. With a deep breath, I go upstairs to check on Billy. He seems distraught. Using his device, I ask him "What do you need?" Billy navigates from "dictionary" to "people" to "family". He proceeds to press each specific relative he has not seen. I ask Billy if he wants to see his uncles and aunts. As he selects the "yes" button, he clicks his tongue and nods. Immediately I confirm that his relatives will visit him. I walk out of his room. I am dumbfounded. Billy is right. He is ill. They live in the greater Cleveland area. Where are they? Matt and I search for answers to alleviate the physical pain and now I must fend off the emotional vicissitudes Billy encounters. Where is my family? Billy is right. Why didn't I extend an invitation? Why didn't I arrange for them to visit with Billy? Have I created an emotional fortress so I can steel myself against any potential breach?

I pace the upstairs hallway. I'm not sure what to do. I move from room to room. I know every corner. I know every angle. I wander downstairs. Talking to myself, I drift in and out of each familiar room. My anxiety is heightened by the fact that I cannot shield my son or myself from the head-on impact. I'm angry that I let Billy down. I'm angry that all of us pigeonhole Billy to suit our own confused aims. How is it possible that we somehow seduced ourselves to believe that Billy would not notice our acts of social omission? My head spins. My thoughts whirl. Has Billy's state of perpetual illness forced me to protect myself to the point that I don't want my siblings to know the magnitude of my grief? I cannot believe that I didn't foresee and acknowledge Billy's need for emotional healing. Anguished and tired, I ask my mother, why they didn't visit Billy? She offers repeatedly to call them. When I ask her again why they didn't visit? My mother says that she doesn't know the answer. She is sad but she is honest. I don't want to make these calls. But I am Billy's mother and I must make these calls. I dial the phone numbers and receive voice recordings.

I am relieved. In a brief, but official manner I relay Billy's message that he would like to see them and was hoping that they'd drop by this afternoon or evening. Thanks. Click. I'm nervous and defensive. Billy harbors no judgment. He just wants them in his life. From Billy's perspective, being at Granny and Grandpa's house means that you are with your family.

Billy understands this. It will take me more time.

It's so awkward for my sisters and me. We would never intentionally mistreat each other or Billy. Billy's inquiry, however, penetrates my mental armor. My reactions surprise me. I'm startled by their blatant absence. It's humiliating to feel so let down. This is uncharted terrain. I'm not myself. Within a minute both of my sisters call back and respond that they will be over. There is no cogent explanation or elaboration as to why they hadn't seen Billy. We all know there is no decent answer. When they arrive, the conversation is stilted but necessary. My emotions are on the fritz. I try to recede into the background as the conversation drones on. I need some breathing room. We settle into the familiar family dynamics that include humor and witty repartees. My sisters are here to see me and to see Billy. That's all we need. Too frail to come downstairs, we go up together in single-file walk into the den where Billy lies on his side enveloped in blankets. Each family member bends down and greets Billy. Billy responds with gratitude etched in his face. The circumstances are new. The emotions are raw and unclear. But the relationships matter.

Two Black Eyes

Going off meds is risky. Going off a seizure medication to try another one is treacherous. It's not just an even swap for one medication for another. It's not an airtight solution. It is a slow withdrawal from the medication that has run havoc on the body for another "unknown" that is administered in measured, incremental amounts. Full dosage takes time. No one is sure what will happen. The transition from one seizure med to another presents grave imbalances in the body. Billy is in limbo. During the switchover, he is not covered for optimal seizure control. It's a dangerous waiting game.

It is August and we are at Cape Cod for the weekend. The season is winding down. The days are shorter. The colors of fall are faint but emerging. College students are heading back to school. Families with young children are buying school supplies. We don't fit those categories. At nineteen, Billy suffers from a seizure condition that has yet to be controlled. He is okay. But he is not well.

Matt and I decide go out for dinner at a nearby Italian restaurant. Shelly, Billy's trusted and loving friend and assistant, joins us on this last Cape weekend. We think Billy is safe. We think we can dine at a table for two on an August Saturday night. The Cape is our summer haven. As we are seated at a window front table with a patio bedecked with summer flowers, we breathe deeply and order our drinks. It is so refreshingly aromatic. The air is filled with soft conversational exchanges and clinking wine glasses. In that moment, it is just Matt and I looking at each other across a white tablecloth-covered table. In a rare yet familiar gesture Matt extends his hands across the table and our hands embrace. He smiles at me adoringly. We are together. At the same time, I hear the vibration sound waves from Matt's blackberry. Hooked on his belt like the doctor on call he has become, he withdraws his hands and answers. Shelly is on the other line. Trying to be reassuring but breathing urgency, she tells Matt that she thinks Billy may have had a seizure. Billy was in the lower level rec room watching a video. The sliding glass doors are dead bolted. The floors are thickly carpeted. But Billy is frail. His physical movements are slower. His communication initiatives are more hesitant. Instead of pointing and pressing the button on his device, his finger hovers. The quick click of the tongue to the upper roof of the mouth Billy stylized years ago to signify yes is barely present. Moving his head left to right, to indicate "no," wanes. We are vigilant in keeping Billy near us at all times. So every three to five minutes Shelly runs down the stairs from the kitchen to check on him. Billy appears content and relaxed as he lies on the sofa watching his nightly video. There are no signs of visible distress.

Matt concludes the call. We get the waitress' attention and inform her that we think our son may have suffered a seizure and that we must leave. We are overly apologetic to the restaurant owner who reassures us that going to our son is first priority. It is an odd existence to tightrope our two realities. Matt and I are engaged in our life together. But we are propelled back to Billy. Almost running Matt and I scurry around the tables of other diners as we exit the restaurant. We live in a split universe.

We arrive back at the house in record time. Sitting on the loveseat slumped over, Shelly's arms shelter Billy as they wait for our return. He is silent, pale, and eerily still. The last time Shelly came downstairs, Billy was on the ground next to the metal banister that leads to the upstairs, awake but disoriented. We conclude that more than likely Billy has suffered a seizure. There is no point in going to the emergency room. We know what the gig is. Matt gives Billy an Ativan and sleeps in the twin bed next to Billy that night. The next morning never happens for Billy. He stays in bed the entire day with two massive black eyes. Billy must have felt the aura sensations and as he tried to ascend the stairs, he seized and hit his head on the white metal banister. I always thought that banisters provided stability. I never saw Billy lying face down in a heap next to the staircase opening. I don't have any tattoos. But I feel like I do. The image of Billy alone, wounded, and unable to secure help is tattooed in my mind. Sometimes the impact of the image softens and the lines blur. It recedes, but it is always with me.

Worn Down
August 2009

I'm exhausted. But it doesn't register. Billy quivers. I grab a Grande Starbucks. I'm exhausted. I work out and do yoga. Billy sobs. I am exhausted. I never pause. Billy wails pain into the early morning hours. I never yawn. Billy succumbs to sleep. I never close my eyes even momentarily. I am hyper-awake.

I don't take naps. Except tonight.

Billy and Ashley are visiting us at the Cape. On cue, we arrive at our favorite restaurant, Abba. The four of us clink our glasses of red wine as we toast cheers. Seated out on the covered terrace, we are a party of four dining revelers. Laughter and storytelling abounds as we savor the food and drink. Content, I nestle my head on Matt's shoulder. Leaning in closer to his warm body, I rest. My eyes open and close as I try to refocus on the softly lit candles and spirited conversation. There is no adrenaline left. I am bone weary. I fall happily asleep. In times of high stress, restaurants and good company are my preferred noise ambiance for slumber.

A Hunch
September 2009

Dr. Buie says he felt something pressing against Billy's intestinal wall. He admits that it is a "hunch". Right now that data point is vital. We have to try something. The simple task of a bowel movement triggers excruciating pain for Billy. Dr. Buie says that he will consult with a surgeon colleague. Medical procedures are sometimes investigative.

As Billy is about to be rolled into the operating room for a laparoscopic appendectomy, he sees that Matt and I are clad in the blue Johnnies. His long medical history suggests that our hospital attire is a familiar sight. What is different are the blue skull hats on top of our heads. No one informed us of the operating-room dress standards. There is no time to craft a social story or to try to communicate via his device about the new hospital protocol. Billy is thrown a curve ball and is not pleased. Straddling each side of the rolling gurney, Billy objects. His intonations are shrill and disapproving; he is visibly distraught. We know exactly what the problem is. I inform the nurse who is pushing Billy in the operating bed that Billy is upset that we are wearing the blue hats. His protestations grow louder and I know if we don't remove the hats, he may not be willing to cooperate with the pending anesthesia administration. In a split second, the nurse motions us to take off the "contraband". Billy calms down instantly. As the double doors open the nurse lets us know that she has a family member with autism. That's the code. Flexibility gets the job done.

I Want to Go Home
October 2009

Our six-hour vigil marking every breath, movement, and twitch ends. Billy stirs but makes no concerted attempt to rise. He turns over and pulls the blanket over his head. He is encased in his white sheets like a mummy from head to toe. The nurse checks in and informs us that Billy must sit up soon to ameliorate the gas pain associated with post-surgery. Matt places two chairs directly next to the bed. Gently I encourage the eyes peeking out of the wrapped sheets to sit next to dad. Barely awake, Billy gingerly moves out of the bed toward the chairs. It is now early evening.

Wrapped in a blanket brought from home, Billy sits on a chair next to Matt. I sit on the other side of the hospital bed that looms in front of us. Groggy from the anesthesia and pain medication, Billy moans, grimaces, and sobs intermittently as he hangs his head down on his chest. He is too distressed from the gas buildup, the surgery, and the ongoing medical probes. This morning's laparoscopic appendix surgery is successful. The medical team's attention and focus moves onto other patients, but Billy's engagement with where he is and what has happened to his body unfolds. For several hours, Billy's face contorts in pain as he grapples with the physical stress. In an effort to connect and comfort him, Matt hands him his device. The device balances precariously on his lap. Finally Billy turns it on and directs his attention to Matt. Review of the upcoming schedule is a welcome reprieve from witnessing my son's emotional wake.

The pediatric overnight recovery unit seems more depressing at night. The bustle of family, visitors, nurses, and doctors making the rounds recedes. The night staff is not as invested in the day's dramatic proceedings. Young and efficient, night-duty nurses knock and inquire about the level of pain discomfort, routinely administer prescribed dosages and monitor patients overnight. The pace is slower, mechanical. At night, the hospital room is lit by fluorescent lighting that showcases the medical paraphernalia circling the bed. It is a stark reality. The TV suspended from the ceiling in front of the bed is set on a comedy station and the hospital dinner arrives. None of these amenities screen out the antiseptic smells, sounds, and hollow ambiance. It's not home.

I'm not sure that Billy will be able to truly rest here. I'm not sure I can rest here. So I go out to the nurses' station and inquire under what conditions it would be advisable for Billy to leave. She tells me that Billy must be awake and he needs to urinate. If he does this in the next hour, she will be able to administer his exit papers. Otherwise, Billy is here for the night. I thank her and tell her that the plan is to leave the hospital tonight and that I'll keep her posted.

As I walk back into Billy's room, I'm not sure how this will play out. Billy and Matt are wrapping up their schedule talk. I don't fully know Billy's medical condition so I'm hesitant to relate to him the nurse's message. I sit back down and observe. Billy is crouched over his device. No one is speaking. We are in recovery and silence is a healing agent. And then I hear his device loud and clear: "I want to go home." His head and neck juts forward and our eyes lock. Billy demands a response. Now I know the answer.

"Billy, first you must use the bathroom and then we can go home."

Billy retorts a resounding "no" on his device as he shakes his head.

"Then we can't go home." I repeat the terms of our exit plan. "Billy, first you must use the bathroom and then we can go home." Billy objects again and vocalizes agitation and declares with dexterous maneuvers on his device. "No."

I cannot concede. The Maginot line drawn, Billy, Matt and I hunker down. There is no deal. Billy stares down at his device and contemplates. An hour passes and then abruptly, as if he'd won the argument, Billy stands and walks majestically into the bathroom and locks the door behind him.

Not knowing what will happen in the bathroom, I'm hell-bent on securing the exit papers. Without hesitation, I announce at the nurse's station that we have our green light and Billy will go home tonight. It takes Billy a good 45 minutes to finally emerge from the restroom. But it doesn't matter. The promise is kept—we head home.

The sky is a clear midnight blue. Billy, Matt, and I huddle together in the driveway and hold each other tight. Billy beams. We are home.

Under the moonlit October sky, Billy turns on his communication device and requests his dinner menu for the evening. It will be a late night. We are off schedule. Billy is back.

A Ray of Light

Billy is on his fourth anti-seizure medication. At what is referred to as therapeutic level, his energy gradually returns. He is nineteen years old and his youth spurs his rejuvenation. Jumping on the trampoline at full tilt, the old Billy is back in action. This is the good news. No, great news!

The bad news is that the new medication—like every other medication—has a multitude of side effects. These generic lists include almost every imaginable human malaise. Liver, heart, or any other potential major organ dysfunction would qualify for immediate cessation. Thankfully, the side effects for Billy are not imminently life threatening. So as long as Billy is pain free, Matt and I are on board.

Here is the issue. Billy cannot initiate sleep. No matter how much exercise, how early he rises, or what natural sleep aid we administer, the young man is on the prowl. Billy's nightlife consists of full-court runs back and forth down our long, narrow hallway. Kitchen detours are also popular. Billy loves big dollops of marshmallow fluff, organic almond butter, and black-cherry jam. The spoons with their sticky remnants are always left neatly by the sink. All crumb trails lead to the cupboard. Chunks of a loaf of challah bread are all that remain. The lights in his bedroom are on and at any point after midnight, I might find Billy sitting in his overstuffed red chair, surveying his domicile "turf".

The festivities end every night between two and three in the morning. This is of course after Matt demands in no uncertain terms that Billy turn off his bedroom lights.

Matt and I try to retire every evening at eleven. Our undying hope is that our consistent and reasonable role modeling will encourage Billy to rethink his nighttime routine. So far, no response from Billy. We are in our third month of sleep deprivation.

As we lie in bed with the fan on high, down the hallway, Billy is just warming up. A few of his finest rebel yells will get the party started. In bed and wide-awake, we try to relax. I toss back cans of sparkling water and Matt tosses, snores, and turns. About two hours later, exhausted, we are on the brink of sleep when a ray of light cascades across our bedroom ceiling. In a state of delirium, I ask Matt what is that light. In an equal state of delirium, Matt pulls the blanket over his head and mumbles that it's just the hallway light.

I know it isn't, but my muddled brain cannot identify the light source. And then I hear the familiar Microsoft tune. Standing in the cracked opening of our bedroom door, Billy's face is awash in the computer light. He looks almost like an ethereal angel. Except this angel is here to seal the deal. At three o'clock in the morning, Billy navigates to all the pertinent pages. As if he is confirming his restaurant reservations, Billy wants one last time our acknowledgment of his Wednesday take-out orders: Dairy Joy for lunch and Papa Razi for dinner. In unison, we pleadingly yell "yes". In an instant, the ray of light is gone and our Billy angel goes to bed with visions of food in his head.

What Do You Think is Going on? October 2009

Billy's doctors confirm that all of Billy pertinent medical records will be available to the medical team on call at Mass General Hospital's emergency room. There are no other options. Billy is extremely ill and self-injurious. In a semi-fetal position, Billy lies very still under the blankets. Only the top of his head peeks out. We arrive by ambulance and are clearing admittance when a doctor who is in charge of the unit holds up her hand and questions our admittance. In midstream to an examining room, we are stopped. The word "autism" is discussed by her and some residents. The doctor in charge assumes that we are headed the wrong way. She assumes that Billy needs to be admitted to the Psychiatric Unit. Overhearing the discussion, Matt interjects and says that Billy's doctors have authorized that Billy's medical issues need immediate attention. His maladies are of a physical nature.

"Don't you have the forwarded paperwork?"

She never directly answers our question. There is a tense pause. At no point in her deliberation does she hear or see Billy. The only information that she has is a visual of a silent young man covered by a blanket from head to toe, and her preconceptions of what type of care someone with the autism diagnosis requires. The doctor also is cognizant of the fact that Matt and I will not stand down. It is awkward, confusing, and humiliating. She whispers something to her colleague and walks away. The EMS medic, Billy, Matt, and I proceed. Billy is wheeled into a drab examination room. He never lifts his head. He never moves. Billy is underground and in this madhouse we need to find answers. The doctor enters, introduces himself, looks at Billy and asks Matt and I a fundamental question. "What do you think is going on?"

179

I already know the answer. I tell the doctor that I believe Billy is having a severe reaction to his current seizure medication. He asks a few questions regarding Billy's behavior and then concurs with my conclusion. As we wait for discharge papers, the attending doctor of the emergency room knocks on the door. I open it and follow her into the hallway. She apologizes for questioning Billy's right to be treated by the ER team. I tell her that I appreciate her candid words. She didn't have to seek me out. No one would have questioned her intentions or actions.

Shutdown

I know what clinical depression is.

Impaled in my brain is this image. It is Saturday afternoon and the sky is dark, saturated by clouds, the air is heavy. It will rain today. But time and weather will soon not matter. Breakfast with Billy is a long-standing, time-honored tradition referred to as the ritual countdown. Our wake-up call commences. In between kitchen tasks, brushing my teeth, putting on mascara, and picking up my clothes, I walk down the hall and enter Billy's bedroom. My fingers held high denote the countdown from ten. I smile and announce like the morning disc jockey the precious numbers left. Barely visible, Billy nods slightly, or clicks with his tongue a confirmation. If I'm too hasty or abrupt, however, Billy argues his case. His hand will emerge from his human shell encasement and correct me by flashing the number of fingers he prefers. As I stand in his doorway clad in my bathrobe and white ankle socks, Billy finalizes his point with a perfectly pitched intonation bordering on a reprimand. Timing is key to the good morning wake-up call. So is patience.

Sipping my coffee I go back to the kitchen and wait for Billy to walk around the corner and announce his grand entrance. Billy's cat run-walks are always colorful, surprising, and unfiltered. Some mornings, he strolls into the kitchen and smiles slyly as we embrace in a bear hug. Other times, he sits down at the kitchen table. Sleepy and chilled, I ask Billy if he wants some "sugar?" Billy grins and nods and I plant a row of kisses on each side of his neck. Then there is the Billy that runs full tilt the length of our bowling alley hallway and then U-turns back and sprints with knees high into the kitchen. With a winner-take-all smile, Billy delivers a raucous good-old-boy high five. In true Billy fashion he checks with radar vision to make sure his device is on and set precisely on the dictionary page. After a few impressive hard jumps in strategically planned spots across the kitchen floor, Billy looks inquisitively outside. He notes the weather status and which cars are parked in the front driveway. Billy is in command and always aware of every maneuver in the house. Interspersed through all his morning rituals is his signature gleeful chuckle that makes anyone smile regardless of his antics. Billy is *Seinfeld's* Kramer.

But this particular Saturday morning is different. Matt is in New York visiting our son Ben who had recently started the NBC Page Program. The original plan was that both Matt and I would go. I was leery. I wasn't convinced that Billy had recovered fully from his reaction to the anti-seizure drug the week prior. Although Billy was informed two days ago about the trip, he still responds like it is first-time news. Changes in his weekend plans are not his strong suit. I expect a minor rumble. After all, Matt is his main buddy and they infamously shop, eat, and carouse at various establishments every Saturday. With device in hand, Billy single-handedly plots the weekend festivities as his dad nods mostly in agreement. These exclusive male-bonding adventures are legendary. I am and always will rate second string on the Saturday lineup. I take another sip of coffee and gird myself for a brief display of emotional fireworks. It is the normal fare. I know what to expect.

And then I don't. As Billy enters the kitchen, I sense a change. I freeze, and every fiber in my body catapults to high alert.

This morning's overture is dark and shadowy. Billy stares at me and not at me and without hesitation he takes his hand to his already wound-infested cheek and begins to gouge. Blood surfaces. His eyes burn fury but at the same time cast a hollow disconnect. The morning routine evaporates and is replaced with a purgatory for the suffering. I yell down to Holly who is downstairs in home school. Holly detects the panic in my voice and runs up the stairs and into the kitchen. She eyeballs Billy and me. Fully aware that Billy responds to a sense of danger, she asks evenly, "What's wrong?"

An overpowering instinct tells me that we have to stop Billy from mauling his face. The stakes are too high. Another emergency-room visit would land Billy in the psychiatric ward. Billy is not psychotic. Billy's state of mind is a direct reaction to the anti-seizure medication Keppra. The doctor informs us that a percentage of young men experience "agitation, aggression, and shutdown" when Keppra levels are increased. I had no idea that on this Saturday morning Billy would derail. That is what shutdown means. For Billy, shutdown means self-flagellation with no exit. I am witnessing Billy shut down.

In that split moment when Holly poses the question and Billy stares at us, raises his hand and digs his flesh, I know that shutdown means that you never leave his side or he will self-implode. My appeals to Billy to listen, to reason, to stop the facial bloodletting are not heard. Our Billy is not present and he cannot control his chemically-charged impulses. Billy does not voluntarily choose to sit. I push and drag him to the purple chair in the family room off the kitchen. Shutdown means that I, his mother, must abandon every nurturing response. I too must shutdown in order to protect Billy from himself. It is physical, brute force and I am the ringleader. Crouched on top of the armrest, I lean my upper body on his chest as my hand pins his right arm and hand. My legs twist around his legs. Stunned, Billy does not immediately break my hold. If Billy does, he bludgeons the sides of his face. With a freed hand he twists and digs his cheeks until the skin rips and bleeds. Billy's face is swollen blue and ghoulish. I lean into his body and fight harder to constrain his movements. I keep my head bowed. I can hardly bear to look at my own son's mutilated face. Holly tries to connect with Billy. She holds down his left hand and looks into the eyes of a stranger. Desperately she beseeches Billy. She counts, hoping that the barely audible succession of numbers will reintroduce the beginning, middle, and end of his torture. Shelly, his friend and companion, kneels at Billy's feet. Her hands fold in prayer. She prays and intermittently caresses Billy's hand as Holly counts. I watch Billy's own dark and watchful eyes stare at these women's unyielding kindness. I am overcome with grief and gratitude. I cannot hold back the tears.

The vigil continues into the early evening hours. Emotionally flatlined, Billy succumbs and goes to his bed. Billy enters his shutdown. Our sole mission is to cut off any stimuli that would cause him to strike himself. We participate in the shutdown. We dim the lights. We leave Billy in isolation. Food and drink are left on the kitchen table, but there is no invitation. Our sole mission is to keep Billy still.

Matt is on his way home from New York. He has left Ben alone in an already paid hotel room with two theater tickets. There is no option. I fear a resurgence of Billy's drug-induced soliloquy of rage. Alone I cannot endure.

It is after midnight. Billy and Matt are asleep. The house is dark. The only noise is the backdrop drone of late-night television. I cannot rest. Billy's acts of aggression and my aggressive response derail my resilient spirit. Curled up on the sofa, I weep and drink Racer Five beers until a wave of numbness temporarily washes away the gravity of the day. This is my shutdown.

Sunday morning is a glorious fall day. The trees brim with autumn colors. In a self-imposed exile, Billy suffers silently in his bedroom. Eyes swollen and my eyelids tinged blue, I take the cup of coffee Matt brings me and we decide to sit out on the back deck while Billy sleeps. Clad in a thin white nightgown and bathrobe, I sit down on a wrought-iron chair and slowly drink my coffee. Matt brings over a chair and sits next to me. Dazed and depleted of any energy reserves, we say nothing. It's been over a year since we sat in our backyard. Billy's myriad of severe maladies limits almost imperceptibly even the mundane routines. Matt and I sit and wait for the doctor's call at noon.

While Matt goes into the house to check on Billy, I stand up and listlessly look around at all the plants that frame our windows. The statuesque Mandevilla, the fragrant jasmine adorned with the white, delicate, feather-light flowers, have withered due to cool autumn evenings. The blooms are gone. All summer I recall admiring their beauty from inside my house. I wrap my robe tighter. Glancing to my right I notice the two gardenia shrubs shaped in a topiary style. My original plan was to sit on the back deck during the summer evenings and enjoy their shiny greenery and the soft, velvet-white flowers that envelop me in aromatic delight. Gardenias conjure southern memories of my childhood in Nashville. As a little girl, I would catch lightning bugs in a glass jar provided by my grandparents. When I got bored, I'd wander around the yard sniffing deeply those white flowers framed in green. The fragrant smells were breathtaking. Now I see the same white velvet flower. I gasp. It is too late. It is too cold. It is not possible. Once more I bend down and inhale the unmistakable scent of the gardenia. In that moment, summer returns in all its vibrancy. I am no longer in lockdown. With the faith of my ancestors, I still am free. I inhale and move forward.

The attending doctor who had seen Billy in the emergency room five days earlier calls us back. He listens as Matt describes the last twenty-four hours. His recommendations are stark yet clear. Billy cannot return to the ER. His manifest symptoms of medical trauma will undoubtedly land him in the psychiatric unit. Hospital protocol overrides the medical realities or the emotional impact on Billy. The doctor concludes that it is not a place for Billy to be. We agree. For the next five days, we sedate Billy, expedite the withdrawal of Keppra and replace it with the new anti-seizure medication. We observe Billy's every movement and wait for his return. During the daylight hours, Billy emerges from his room only to use the bathroom or scavenge for liquids from the refrigerator and food left out on the kitchen table. Billy knows we are there but he makes no attempt to interact. He lives in a dead zone. The episodes of aggression toward himself or others slowly recede. Our home is the recovery unit. There is no viable alternative.

Neosporin Spray

For Billy, the side effects of the anti-seizure medication Keppra trigger a domino reaction. For a small percentage of young adult men in their early twenties, Keppra can cause agitation, aggression, and shutdown. For Billy, the aggression includes force against himself. Every time he stands up from his bed, he attacks his face. Staring straight at me, this person I do not know grabs his facial skin with such brute force that the gouge velocity strips the skin from his upper and side cheeks. Every incident signals a bloody domestic altercation. No one is spared. Everyone involved bleeds.

Domestic triage is never reported but it happens. There is no other way to salvage Billy's self-inflicted facial wounds. Any cream or antibiotic ointment application will unhinge Billy. His sensory system cannot withstand the composition of any gel, cream, or ointment on any part of his body. So I have no choice. Bearing my entire body weight on my twenty-year-old son's ailing body and soul, I spray.

I count and I hold him down with every fiber of my being. This should not be a mother's role but it is mine. Without the Neosporin spray and the narcotics that keep him sedated, Billy will never be released from this drug-induced nightmare.

A Tiny Nail Protrudes
November 2009

A minute nail protrudes barely on the step next to the banister. It is painted the same gold tone of the risers. Blending into the woodwork, it is invisible to most human beings. But not to Billy. Sleep-deprived, Billy teeters on the verge. Still dressed in pajamas, Billy's posture is slack and his eyelids are heavy. Nothing appears normal. Nothing appears right. It is the early afternoon. Billy has not had breakfast. There is no schedule anchoring the time of day. Every day is out of sync. As his finger moves slowly toward the nail, Billy identifies the source of imperfection. He will not move until the nail is pounded into the step. We must fix it.

Friday Night at the Symphony Hall

Always a gentleman, Matt lets me off on Boylston Street. I walk into the side entrance and up the right staircase to cocktail hour. It has been two interminable weeks since Billy hovered on the brink of mental delirium and physical wreckage. Keppra is gradually being replaced with Lamictal. This is our fourth attempt to find an effective and safe anti-seizure medication. I feel the crisis has abated and I need a release from my home, which transformed into a bona fide MASH unit. Leaning against the corner of the mahogany bar, I order a cold Amstel Light and savor the drink, the dignified pre-symphony milling, and the light banter streaming throughout the reception room. I think nothing. My mind delights in the luxury of the moment. I turn my head toward the door and I see Matt walking briskly toward me with his cell phone suspended in air.

I know before Matt speaks. His body language is tragically reminiscent. Billy had a grand mal seizure. His body needs the anti-seizure medicine and can no longer tolerate the depletion. There are no words exchanged between Matt and me, only rapid motion toward the car garage. En route Matt tells me that the EMS team will wait until we get home even though Billy is okay and resting on the sofa. I am incredulous. We may not be home for another thirty minutes. Their consideration for Billy's complex medical condition floods my senses with relief and astonishment. Matt whips into the driveway.

It is a pleasantly cold November night but my house is lit up like a Christmas tree. The emergency response is a triage EMS, police, and firemen. We hasten up the front-deck stairs and open the door to a sea of concerned, tough-guy responders who have Billy's back. Most of them have been to the house before and have come to know Billy. Billy sits at the farm table dazed but scanning something on his device. The guys are seated at the table with Billy and if I blinked I could imagine them being friends. They share his bravado and lust for life. One of the younger EMS guys says, "Oh, I was here in May when Billy accidentally put his arm through the barn window."

Billy is tough. In this kitchen on this post-autumn night is a collection of strangers who express admiration, concern, and love. Billy is no longer a 911 call, he is Billy. As they depart, one of the police officers reassures me and says that when we hear 321, we know and we will be here. I stand outside beneath the star-studded sky surrounded by these *Cheers* characters, humbled by their simple outreach. The fire chief asks me to sign the obligatory paperwork and as I fumble to read the print, he offers me his reading glasses. Well, it isn't a grand night at the symphony, but it is a grand occasion with a star-studded cast.

Love and Suffering
Thanksgiving 2009

It is the second consecutive Thanksgiving that Billy will not celebrate with his family. Billy's acute reaction to the drug Keppra and the ensuing withdrawal catapults him into another medical nightmare. Although no longer held hostage to the psychotic reality of a "shutdown," Billy is ill and weak. He lives the life of a shut-in, a convalescent. For the fourth time, Billy must start a new anti-seizure medication. In order to minimize the likelihood of an adverse reaction, the prescribed uptake for this particular medication is methodically slow. This cautious approach is prudent. Without therapeutic coverage in the interim, however, Billy is barraged by misfiring electrical impulses that bludgeon his body and spirit. Sub-clinical seizures lack the terror and crisis of a grand mal, but the impact is pungent.

In the midst of these endless cycles of pain, Billy fires back at himself and others. Neurological misfires multiply and so do counter acts of aggression toward himself and the individuals he loves dearly. Ritual patterns that once allowed him to seamlessly cope and manage daily changes and transitions have short-circuited. The new hourly ritual patterns are now intense and threatening. These new rituals do not serve as transitions. The new rituals consume his reality. Billy's physical discord becomes ours. If Billy dismantles our appearances by constantly taking off jewelry, glasses, hats, and headbands, his fear and confusion become ours. For Matt and me, the physical acts of passively fending Billy off and loving him take their toll. These ritual aberrations are a burden to Billy, he emotionally and physically deteriorates.

The week of Thanksgiving, Billy is listless. He spends his days in bed in a room devoid of light and ventures outside his room only to use the toilet. Once or twice Billy wanders down the hall to stare at the familiar but now dissonant sights, sounds, and smells of holiday preparations. The gathering of relatives for a sumptuous feast and raucous merriment is met by a young man in pajamas, slumped and placid. Billy is alone and ill on this Thanksgiving Day.

> Want what you have
> Do what you can
> Be who you are
> – Rev. Forrest Church
> *Love and Death: My Journey through the Valley of the Shadow*

This mantra is grounded in blood, sweat, and tears but abundant in human possibilities. This Thanksgiving, I choose this excerpt to read as my prayer of hope, faith, and love for my family and for Billy. Together in the kitchen at the farm table, we congregate. I am at the head of the table near the hallway entrance. Solemnly, I begin to read. No one hears him walk down the hall toward the kitchen. Like an apparition, Billy hovers over my back and holds in each hand my dangling pierced chandelier earrings. I hear stunned silence, gasps, and I scan unknowing fear in my family's eyes. With his strong calloused hands, he is physically capable of ripping them from my ears. I don't believe that Billy seeks vengeance. I believe that Billy seeks connection in the midst of his suffering. Motionless, my hands hold each side of the book. I cannot see his face. I only feel the weight and heat of his clasped hands. Billy releases his grip and walks out of the kitchen into the dark hall that leads to his bedroom.

Billy's act of aggression on me in front of his beloved family is an act of communication. Of suffering and love. Thanksgiving evening, Billy and I live the mantra:

Want what you have
Do what you can
Be who you are
Billy did not miss Thanksgiving. He participated as best he could. Amen.

The Missing Gold Earring Christmas 2009

Our car is parked in a parking lot with a rest area that arches over the highway just outside Buffalo, New York. It is December, two days before Christmas. The wind whips and the air temperature is frigid and I am on my hands and knees next to the car. My hands are burning cold and I am angry as I scavenge through our car trash bag that was on the backseat floor when my gold dangle earring went flying. It's Billy's fault. Daily he exacts retribution. I also know it's not his fault. Billy and I are both unhinged. Pain is the culprit. Without warning, Billy unleashes. From the backseat of the car, he lunges at my earring and jolts off the gold post. The force of his swipe catapults the earring somewhere in the car. And now Billy insists upon reconciliation. He wants to make amends. Gazing directly at me, he will not stop pointing solicitously to my remaining earring. I want Billy to stop his gestures of goodwill. I just want him to be quiet so I can decompress. There will be no pause. No downtime to regroup. Billy needs me. Crouched over the passenger seat, Billy watches intently as I dump the remains of the garbage bag on the ice-patched cement in a last-ditch effort to locate the missing earring. The gold dangling earring must be found and returned to my ear. Billy's vocalizations are tinged by the mire of desperation. No matter the egregious act, family harmony must prevail. Billy swiped it off my ear. And I can't find it. My fingers are numb. I throw the bag back into the backseat, get back into the car and snap at Matt to start driving. I unlock my seatbelt, turn around on my knees and face Billy. "Billy, the gold earring is gone." In an effort to quell his mounting stress over the lack of closure, I remove the other gold dangling earring. There is nothing more I can do. There is nothing more Billy can do. We drive to Cleveland for Christmas, burdened by our humanness.

In the early evening, we arrive in Cleveland. The driveway is dark but the sight of my parents' jubilant faces behind the lit back door is my angel choir. We do not travel light. Billy brings at least five plastic bags that contain clothes, toiletries, three CDs, animals, and highly preferred blankets, the puffy kind that do not squish flat. Matt and I are no better. The kitchen floor is covered in our personal provisions. My dad, perched on a stool holding a glass of full-bodied Cabernet, affectionately chuckles and asks if we plan to stay a month! Her Christmas apron on, my mother stands in the middle of the mounting debris and beams, happy we all arrived safely. The jostling, the kisses, the camaraderie are the antidote from the road just outside Buffalo. Billy, Matt, and I missed last Christmas. Billy was too ill and in too much pain: we all suffered. So a year later Billy tepidly reacquaints himself with his grandparents' house. Every room and every level is chalked with his childhood memories. The third floor is where Billy, Ben and their first cousins Alex and Matt have always presided. It is the young masters' quarters and Billy has always loved the boy's shenanigans, loud music, and friendship.

This Christmas Billy drifts past his cousins as if they are total strangers. Upon entering the living room, he pauses, touches and gazes at each family photo displayed as if he is seeing them for the first time. He glances at the vivid sparkling lights and resplendent ornaments of the Christmas tree and then averts his eyes and bows his head. The place, this season, are ghosts from Christmas pasts. The Billy of Christmases past is nowhere to be found this night.

Billy, Matt, and I are not downstairs with the family. Instead we follow Billy upstairs as he unpacks his bags and places his belongings in their proper place. Organized, we assume Billy will follow his schedule, which is to first take a shower and then eat dinner. After his grooming rituals, we will go back downstairs and join the others. The anticipated progression of events never takes place. Billy, Matt, and I are stuck upstairs. We want to be downstairs, but we are stuck upstairs. The festivities flourish on the first floor, a staircase away. But the merriment is unobtainable. Billy is lost. On his fourth anti-seizure medication, Billy is not at what the doctors refer to as the "therapeutic level". Billy is stuck and his medical reality is our reality. Disoriented, Billy cannot move forward. He cannot take a shower. He cannot eat dinner. His fluent understanding and relish for the rapid clip of activities has vanished. The schedule ceases to bear meaning. Billy, Matt, and I stand in the hallway; there is no exit. I'm not sure what recourse we have. And so for me, Billy following the "schedule" becomes all consuming. Blocking the stairwell with my body, I point to the bathroom. No response. No response. No response. An hour passes and fatigue fuels my desire for Billy to take a shower. Without the shower as the kick start, Billy, Matt and I are in a perpetual holding pattern. Will Billy ever eat? Will Billy ever sleep? At this moment Billy is lost. Every crease in his face is anxiety driven. His inability to move forward angers and scares me.

I cannot accept this. The image of my forlorn Billy and the sounds of laughter downstairs are unbearable. I want to join my parents downstairs in the dining room. I need the schedule as much as Billy. I am no longer reasonable. Distraught, I push his strong shoulders in the direction of the bathroom yet he is immovable. I look at Matt and tell him that he must wait with Billy. I leave. I too, like Billy, cannot forge ahead. I feel cornered. My exit is ill timed. I am a deserter.

Christmas Eve

It is mid-afternoon on Christmas Eve. Carefree, Billy's cousins and Ben gather in Granny's kitchen. Between horseplay, breakfast, and marathon viewing sessions of football matches, they are now casually putting on their coats and heading out for the annual workout before the holiday feast. Billy cannot join them. Still in his pajamas, listless and stooped in the kitchen chair, Billy stares at his breakfast. It is 2 p.m. Every mundane activity is an inordinate struggle to start, do, and complete. His exceptionally swift and expeditious movements through the day are now heavy, slow, and at times confusing. Billy's pain bludgeons all his natural exuberance. There are no wisecrack smiles. There are no search-and-find missions to locate and consume all desserts. There is no studious inventory of the refrigerator's culinary delights. There are no embraces or high fives to his cousins. There are no cuddles with Ben. Billy languishes while Ben and his cousins thrive in a state of youthful vitality. Like in Dickens's *A Christmas Carol*, I too fall to the ground and beg that this vision of Christmas future be stricken from the book. But this will not happen. Billy and I know the line between lightness and darkness and it is our Christmas to celebrate.

Hitting the Wall
January 2010

Home school is in the lower level of our home. At basement level, there are four small windows where daylight filters in. Recessed lights and Billy's paintings hang on every available wall. It is a hang-out space. Since the age of eighteen, however, Billy's entire educational and social milieu has revolved in this subterranean basement. This morning, at the age of 20, Billy descends the stairs to home school. It is the longest distance he can trek safely. It is the only transition in his day. It is a tab on his schedule that he moves over to the finished column. All the other tabs denoting his endeavors are archived or barely existing. Gymnastics is gone. Skiing is gone. Ice skating is gone. Workouts are gone. Jumping on the trampoline is gone. Swinging into the rafters of his beloved barn is gone. Swimming is gone. Computer activities are gone. Going to his carefully selected restaurants is gone. There are no vacations. There are no weekend excursions. There are no more special occasions. There are no more present or future anticipations.

Home school is the last holdout. It is his only destination. An emotional hospice, home school is no longer where Billy calls the shots and communicates with glee when he presses the Speaking Dynamically Pro voice output button on his device that he "changed his mind." Home school is no longer where Billy jokes around, swaggers, works hard, and loves. It is an emotional enclave where he receives attention, connection, and encouragement from Holly and David, teachers, and friends who believe that the robust Billy will return with time. Home school is the only physical break from a cycle of pain. With two or three comforters, Billy lies down on the sofa and covers his body in a tight cocoon. Time stands still. There is no agenda. If it is humanly possible, Billy paints colors on a canvass or practices restorative yoga in reclining poses with weighted blankets covering his body. The sessions are short and sparse. No one complains. No one objects. This is reality. Billy endures. We all endure.

199

And then there was that one home-school day when all of us felt endurance would not sustain Billy or the team. With his device in hand, Billy walks over to the table and plugs in his Toughbook. There is no green light. Billy's communication device does not turn on. Smudged with leftover pasta sauce, the screen remains blank. Again he pushes the lever to the right. The screen is dark. His lips quiver and tears well in his eyes. Billy unplugs the device and carries it to Holly and places it on the desk where she sits in front of her laptop. Facing each other, the device is positioned between them. For a moment there is no sound or movement. It is the beginning of home school. Billy gulps breath and grasps Holly's forearm. Tilting his head in an inquisitive mode, Billy concentrates on Holly's response to his broken device.

Holly repeats the technical checklist that Billy has already tried. There is no change. Incredulous, Billy's cheek muscles spread wide, his forehead tightens and his eyeballs flash wide as his eyelids lower as a way to deflect the fact that Holly cannot fix the device. Billy does not move. He is watchful as Holly tries to convince him that the device will be fixed. The technical glitch is a temporary disruption. She writes him a note that indicates that although this device is impaired, he could use his backup communication device. Pointing to each word, Holly reads him the message. Billy crushes the note and discards it in the trashcan. The note is meaningless. Holly then shows Billy the box it came in and encourages him to slide the device in so that it can be mailed to the manufacturer for repair. Billy gulps deep breaths and again gently grabs Holly's forearm pleading for a simple solution. Holly confides to Billy that this "sucks". Billy stops listening. With the device and power cord in hand, Billy plugs the device into every electrical outlet he can find. Straining to keep her own emotions in check, Holly witnesses Billy's unraveling.

Holly writes another note that states the facts. "Device broken, fix later." Billy swipes the note out of Holly's hands, wads it into a crinkled ball and drops it on the table. There are no more communication attempts by Holly or Billy. Holly sits at her desk. The mailing box for the device is on the desk. Billy sits in his orange chair. He moans, and rocks his upper body. There is nothing left to say. There is nothing left to do. Four hours later, Billy approaches Holly, hesitates and then motions with a glance to the cardboard box. Billy observes Holly slide his device into the box and close it shut. It is ready for shipment. Home school has officially ended. Billy hooks up his back-up device and sits down in his orange chair. Staring off into space, Billy breathes hard and fast. With no warning signal, Billy leaves home school and goes back to his bedroom to take another break.

Late in the afternoon, I go downstairs to confer with Holly. She sits at her desk with her back crouched over some papers. I move the porcelain garden stool over and join her. There are few words shared. Just backed-up streams of tears. That day the line between communication and chaos was too thin.

I asked Holly to write about her experiences with Billy that morning the device failed. She wrote:

Sad, scared, overwhelmed, fearful, and anxious are just a few words to describe how I felt during and after our ordeal. I can't imagine how Billy felt. I'd imagine he felt the same way. I'd imagine he feels that way on some level every day. For the first time, I felt like I couldn't connect with Billy. For the first time, I think I felt what Billy has felt throughout his life as he has struggled and learned to connect, communicate, and form relationships with friends and family.

Sage Speech
February 2010

On Thursday, I announce to Billy that he will return to gymnastics. Holly has written a social story explaining his victorious return. Almost giddy that Billy can finally resume a historically poignant part of his life, I fail to realize the message from Billy's point of view. For the last two years, Billy's workouts have disappeared due to grand mal seizures, surgeries, and pain. It has been a full year since Billy has set foot in the Massachusetts Gymnastic Center where he spent ten years of his life. Billy still experiences pain. The pain episodes, however, are not ever-present. For now Billy is better. I'm concerned about his physical health but also his mental state of mind. I think he needs to return to pieces of his former life. Increments. Billy needs to see Patrick, his gymnastics coach. It's not about the workout. It's about friends. Their bond is based upon trust and respect. More importantly, they will receive each other with open arms.

Finding Patrick was fortuitous. Twelve years ago I made a cold call to the gym, inquiring about after-school programming. The person on the receiving end handed the phone over to the director. I explained that my son Billy was on the autism spectrum and asked if he would consider giving Billy private gymnastic lessons. Without hesitation, Patrick agreed. At the age of eight, Billy and I showed up at the gym. It was a shaky beginning. Billy loved his trampoline at home and immediately bee lined to the one at the gym. With confidence and glee Billy jumped with abandon. None of the other gymnastic equipment, however, interested Billy. The trampoline captivated his sensory system. Heights elated him. Jumping gave his body feedback and freedom. All the other apparatus was unfamiliar and thus suspect. Billy would not budge from the trampoline. With the gymnastic schedule sequencing a photograph of each piece of equipment in one hand and clutching screaming Billy's hand, each week I dragged Billy to one new station. Maybe. Inevitably, Billy would "escape" and run back to the trampoline. Full retreat. Most sane adults would have thrown in the towel. Billy howled and Patrick smiled. I was energized.

United, we tried again. Our steps were small and that was just fine. Patrick would demonstrate at each station what was possible. Billy would observe. And then, slowly and deliberately, we broke down each gymnastic maneuver to a series of sequential steps that Billy felt comfortable trying. Other lessons unfolded: keen observation, trust in others, self-pride, and self-pacing. Gradually Billy learned the meaning of pause. The correlation of breathing and rest became meaningful. As Billy entered the middle-school years, he became a skilled negotiator on the number of times he would repeat an exercise. Billy would propose a number by the count of fingers he displayed, and Patrick would counter with his finger spread in turn. By his high-school years, he had mastered a handstand spring over the vault as well as a reverse handstand on the rings. Back handsprings were practiced weekly. As Billy propelled his body up and backwards, he could not see the endpoint. With Billy willing to face the "blind spot," Patrick became his spotter and Billy trusted him unequivocally. They were allies. Billy was a bona fide gymnast. Billy was strong. Gymnastics was his sport. Machismo was his game.

Naively, I think Billy is "well". From a medical standpoint, his physical symptoms have abated. The healing process, however, has just begun. On the computer, Holly crafts a social story, which documents new information through visual symbols, photos and correlating text. As a visual communicator, Billy's "language" requires that communication partners utilize a visual system to convey their feedback. Due to the visual format, social stories allow Billy the time to process the information and refer to it for further clarification.

But visual, text, and verbal dissemination of the information doesn't guarantee full comprehension or automatic acceptance. This social story informs Billy that because he is better, it is time to go back to Massachusetts Gymnastics Center and reunite with his coach Patrick. I think he will be elated. Within seconds of reading it together, Billy grabs the paper, crumbles it, and tosses it into the trashcan. I am concerned but not deterred. I've witnessed such dramatic gestures endless times. Billy is not fond of disruptions in his daily schedule.

The next morning I try again. I walk into Billy's room, pull up the shade and say good morning. As is the custom, I announce the day and the activities that are planned. At the end of my morning news announcements, I herald the fact that Billy will return to gymnastics. Fiercely, he shakes his head. No. Stunned by Billy's emotional objection, I hesitate to retort. Stumbling but optimistic, I reiterate my announcement. Billy vigorously repeats "No". His head whips back and forth as his neck muscles contract and his face rages red against the suggestion. And then I remember a book I've just read. An accomplished artist is blinded in his New York apartment due to a break-in scuffle. One of the words he uses to describe how it felt to re-learn to walk down a New York street was "fear". Fear arrests the movement forward. And then I realize that my son Billy habors fear. Fear paralyzes Billy's ability to aspire.

"Billy, are you afraid to go back to gymnastics?"

Clicking his tongue between his teeth, Billy says "Yes". But this yes is not a yes to a need or a response to a factually based question. This yes is an emotional admission that I've never witnessed. I run to the kitchen, grab his device and run back to his room. Sitting on the bed beside my son, Billy navigates to a page and with sad determination he presses the button "No" and moves to his red chair as if to say that the conversation is finished.

With device in hand, I too move and sit on the edge of the red chair. Quietly, almost in whisper tones, I say, "Billy I know you are afraid but you love gymnastics. Don't you want to see Patrick?"

Quivering tears, Billy dismisses the notion with a flick of his hand.

Navigating to the "friends" page, I point to the photo of Patrick and I say, "Billy, Patrick is your friend."

I hear Billy's faint click of affirmation.

"Billy, Patrick loves you and you love Patrick."

Another tongue click.

"Billy you do not need to be afraid. You will see your friend Patrick and gymnastics will be "easy". That was our code word for "you can do this."

But this return to gymnastics conjures a minefield of emotions.

Billy's life drought has been long and arduous. What does it mean to go back to gymnastics? Maybe Billy recognizes that he is not the same person who left gymnastics. Physically, his left bicep bears multiple, jagged scars from an extreme reaction to a prescribed medication for seizures. Billy's history of physical pain would make any sane person question the legitimacy of my proposal. His body mass smaller, Billy no longer oozes muscle swagger.

To revisit the possibility of going back to gymnastics means that he can no longer sublimate the psychological trauma he endures.

When we enter the Massachusetts Gymnastics Center, it is a homecoming. Patrick receives Billy with arms wide open. On the verge of deserved tears, Billy enfolds himself into Patrick's embrace like a young warrior who comes home and harbors painful, unspeakable memories. Billy surveys the wide-open gym. He walks the circumference of the gym, pressing his feet on the gym mats and tentatively touching all the gymnastic equipment that his body had once maneuvered with dynamic precision.

Another passage, another learning curve.

Rock-and-Roll Billy
March 2010

Monday morning, Billy and I review the social story about a new doctor's visit. Social stories provide Billy with the narration and pivotal visuals that inform him of what the changes in the schedule entails. Having a visual reference for the day's events alleviates his anxiety and enhances his understanding of the beginning, middle, and end of what will transpire, enabling Billy to be flexible and confident. Holly takes a picture of the fairly innocuous, suburban brick building as a way to visually emphasize the fact that this trip is primarily a consultation and not a bona fide medical visit. In other words, Billy will not undergo any medical procedures. We emphasize the difference between a consult visit and a medical visit, and reassure him that the doctor will only examine his eyes, ears, and throat. The social story summarizes the medical event as an "easy visit".

Historically, this "easy visit" pitch does not always assuage Billy's fears. Billy's ongoing pain and discomfort generate a lower tolerance for schedule disruptions and new information or activities. Acute pain often dissolves any element of trust in the social-story display. Billy's survival instincts for fight or flight are formidable. I brace myself for a rip-roaring showdown in the kitchen, in the car, and yes, maybe at the doctor's office.

But I am wrong. I am wrong about Billy. Not once does it occur to me that Billy's response to a difficult request might change. This Monday morning, armed with the social story, I steel myself for controversy, for the same response, not for greater insight or transformation on Billy's part. But Billy is a communicator and communication is fluid and evolving, never static. Adults learn, change, and grow. Why should Billy's life be different? Years of physical duress and emotional trauma compounded by an array of medical procedures have had a profound impact on Billy's sense of self. Pain and all its accompanying emotions are a deeply personal and visual experience that he knows, identifies, and expresses through his language-device system. Billy understands why he needs medical help.

Billy trusts the message and the person who delivers it. Emotional and social confusion happen daily and in sync. Emotional and social maturation unfold. I am not a mind reader.

Perhaps I, too, suffer from "mind blindness".

So that Monday afternoon, Matt, Holly, Billy, and I go to the suburban medical office building. We file into the doctor's office. Four chairs are positioned in front of the doctor's imposing desk. We take our seats. The laptop stationed in front of him, the doctor begins his inquiry. Our social discourse is awkward. His eyes dart up to pose his questions. But as soon as Matt or I answer, he focuses entirely on the screen. This question-and-answer disconnect period drones on for almost an hour. In an almost Zen-like practice, Billy sits erect with his palms resting lightly on his thighs. He dons the black Ray Bans and there appears to be a slight smile on his lips. Billy is serene and we are at a new medical facility with a doctor he has never met. And then the doctor stops typing his write-up on the computer. He swivels his chair toward Billy, glances at him, and directs his question to us: "Is he light sensitive, or a rock-and-roll star?"

I answer proudly, I think the latter.

Rock on Billy.

Barium X-Ray
April 2010

Just because you have the social story doesn't mean you won't encounter glitches. Billy clears his throat after every meal. I don't really mean, "clears" his throat. There is no proper word to depict the full-body-propelling tilt combined with the sound of a violent yet unsuccessful guttural purge. This monumental throat vibration will at the very least inflame his entire esophageal tract. Although I am sorely attempted to downplay the daily occurrence, a proper investigation can no longer be "put on hold." It's a medical puzzle that needs to be solved. Why does Billy insist, day after day, on conducting such a grating exercise? What purpose does it serve? Does this communication behavior imply an undetected source of pain? No one can answer that question without performing some tests. One of the tests we decide to try is a barium swallow. So armed with some facts and Googled research, Holly and I piece together as best we can what will actually take place.

Prior to our visit, Billy reviews the social story. The narrative written by me informs Billy that the test is like an X-ray except with liquid drinks. He knows that he will sit, drink this barium cocktail, and then lie down on the table and wait for the X-ray. It is couched as an "easy" test. What Billy doesn't know is that the radiology team will direct him to lie down on the machine and sip from a straw in a supine position. Billy growls. This content was not included in his social story because we didn't know and no one bothered to inform us. The medical team, however, assumes immediately that Billy's reaction means that he doesn't care for the taste or the texture of the drink. For some individuals on the autism spectrum, this conclusion might be accurate. But not in Billy's case. No one likes an unexpected switch in the game plan and neither does Billy! What gets him irked is the unrehearsed deviation from the social story. Or better known as the "deal". So Billy vocalizes adamantly his disapproval.

No problem. But then they inform me that Billy needs to move from his back to his side. The visual and the text denoting the "side" of the body is in the carefully constructed social story, but it doesn't matter. Pointing to the specifics in the social story or telling him to turn on his side does not translate! For Billy, I'm speaking a foreign language. Billy is baffled and a bit impatient. So I do what I've done so many times—I "ad-lib". Determined to complete successfully this barium-swallow exam, I make eye contact with Billy and say, "Do this". With my radiation-proof vest wrapped and tied around my torso, I lie down on my side on the cold floor and look up at Billy on the X-ray table. Billy understands my interpretation and without further ado, turns on his side. Yes, we complete the test. More importantly, Billy is spared the frustration and social humiliation that signifies a breakdown in communication.

The dilemma is that the doctor who authorizes the test is not the doctor who will conduct it. Doctors are dedicated and engaged in their patients' care specific to their expertise. The current system, however, is not designed to value the time required for doctors to communicate to referred doctors about the patients' communication issues and needs. Neither is there time slated to assess and communicate to the family all the steps involved in any given procedure. Billy and all his compatriots need to know the facts. Knowing what will take place, in what order, and when it will be finished clinches the deal.

Understanding Intent

We've just arrived to see a new neurologist. The doctor is pleasant, observant, and focused on documenting the information. Her computer is on and her fingers are poised to record. Billy is not well. This is clear. His face is puffy and flushed. His eyelids are heavy. He shouldn't be here. But we have an appointment and we need to meet with the doctor and introduce Billy. As Matt, Holly, Billy, and I congregate in her office, there occurs a commotion that lasts a split second. Billy opens his satchel with his device inside and situates it on the round table. Placement of coats, purses, and seating configurations are in motion. I'm about to sit down when Billy gains eye contact with me. His gaze is edged in illness and distress. As I register his state of mind, Billy grabs my pierced earrings. He does not want to be in this medical space. In the same sweeping motion he releases his hands. The doctor observes and types with authority that Billy exhibits aggressive behavior toward his mother. No questions are posed about the interaction. Only conclusions that are inaccurate are recorded. I silently cringe.

Billy Deserves an Answer - July 2010

It is a shimmering July afternoon and I am in Dr. Buie's windowless office. I don't want to attend another medical appointment for Billy. I feel like I am in a never ending revolving office door. Too many entrances and exits. I'm spent. I don't know how much more I can do. The sounds and visuals morning, noon, and night of Billy's acute physical stress drains me. My optimism is splintered. I can't imagine what we could possibly do next. But I know I should be in this office. The doctor needs to know what is going on. Billy's throat clearing remains constant, all day and night. The act of swallowing is a harrowing ordeal. Billy's solution is to drink and eat as fast as he can. In his mind, less time equals less powerful pressure on his esophagus.

It doesn't work. Throat clearing and reflux combine forces. After eating he stands up and exhausts every throat muscle as he struggles to extinguish the tightness, pressure, and reflux. He propels his arms and bellows. Nothing works. Dr. Buie listens, squints his eyes, folds his arms, and leans back on the rolling desk chair. The story, in his professional opinion, mandates another upper GI scope with biopsies. I'm taken aback by the doctor's conclusion. Perhaps I thought that just relaying the story would be sufficient. I did my job by reporting the facts. And then I would walk out of the air-conditioned office building into the late summer day. Off the hook. I did not want to go back into the hospital. I object and counter and that maybe we should wait. Was it really necessary? Dr. Buie looks at me across the round table at which we have spent endless hours reviewing Billy's litany of medical issues and tells me that after all of his travails, "Billy deserves an answer." His answer is compassionate and resolute.

I am not prepared to hear the answer. But it is so right.

Are You Going to the Grocery Store?

The night before Billy's fifth colonoscopy, Matt strips the kitchen of all possible foods that Billy, the night cruiser, could ransack in the middle of the night. We take no chances. The last thing we need to hear is that his intestinal tract isn't clear enough to make an accurate determination. Oh no. Not on our watch! All condiments, fruits, deserts, breads, Tums, vitamins, anything that Billy might ingest in the final hours are confiscated and locked in the front closet. The cupboards are bare and the refrigerator is stripped of all consumable temptations.

That evening after the kitchen purge, Billy walks in and in his daily practice inspects all the food-holding receptacles. He is informed that his procedure is tomorrow. But the new and improved Billy, who has four colonoscopies under his belt, does not push the panic button. There are no demonstrative outbursts.

No, Billy is Cool Hand Luke. He strolls over to his device, navigates to the page "Billy's Questions," and asks Matt on his device a perfectly logical question. "Dad, are you going to the grocery store?" Billy's demeanor is completely stress-free. And Matt's? Not so much.

Fifth Colonoscopy
August 2010

Billy sits up in his double bed. On first glance as I walk past his bedroom, Billy at the age of twenty looks so healthy and debonair as he slowly wakes up. His facial expression, however, is different this morning. Introspective. His eyes gaze inwardly focused on a distant point, Billy appears thoughtfully resolved. I sit close beside him and our hands clasp gently. Billy's hands are calloused, dry and warm. Our hands intertwined are our trust line. Holding hands, I inform Billy that it is time to go to the hospital and the doctor will help Billy's stomach pain. Our silent pauses, our embrace are the human antidote to the maze of medications and procedures.

Street clothes on, including his Nike Shox sneakers and double-layered socks, Billy sits upright in the hospital bed divided by a flimsy curtain wall on either side of his berth. He waits, fully aware of what is about to take place. He observes Matt and me answering the nurse's questions about the anesthesia protocol and he hears us remind the nurse that Billy stays dressed, does not wear an ID band, and responds to number counts by us when the time comes for the needle injection. He glances at Holly standing by the side of his bed, reassuring him in ways that only best friends can. In front of him is a visual panorama of hospital fare. Nurses are on the computers, a child on a gurney escorted by his parents wheels past Billy's curtained but open space. On the right side adjacent to Billy's bed, a doctor discusses the medical issues with a young female patient. The room is filled with monitors, drip bags, bright lights, and constant movement.

Despite the flurry of medical drama unfolding before him, Billy is not perturbed. In a quiet way, Billy reaches for his device and navigates to the main dictionary page and then to the page entitled family. He presses the Speaking Dynamically Pro buttons that speak, "I want to see Ben." A young, twenty-year-old man who cannot "speak" seeks out the love and support of his brother in his time of unfathomable duress. In a hospital bed waiting for his turn, Billy's personal act is so grounded. No other sound makes sense.

Magnesium Citrate

With an air of civility, Billy leads me to the kitchen cabinet and opens the cherry-paneled door. He stoops down and points to the back of the shelf beyond Annie's organic split pea soup. Gently, he shifts his attention to me and inquires with his touching gaze. It could not have been clearer. Billy asks that the magnesium citrate be removed. The colonoscopy is finished. What a gentleman! I would have ranted and raved.

Ode to Joy — Fall 2010

It happens every morning in the bathroom. Seated on a toilet seat clad in Matt's Hanes white underwear shirt and black nylon Nike running pants, and in between brushing his teeth and washing his face, there occurs thirty seconds of Billy's "ode to joy." There is no fanfare. There is no audience. There are no cameras. In the midst of pain, disorientation and unknowing, there are fleeting glimpses of lightness. In those instances, Billy's spirit flourishes.

And there are no earthly reasons that would adequately explain Billy's daily expressions of unadulterated joy. Its origins are illogical, even mystical. Every night Billy eats his dinner and every night his body convulses in pure, uninterrupted pain. Running his hands rapidly through his hair, screaming and sobbing, he sits on the living room sofa and rocks until he can bear the spasmodic esophagus assaults on his body. Even his unrelenting raw and penetrating throat clearing cannot thwart this allergic reaction to food. Food signifies nourishment, pleasure, comfort, and health. Billy eats his dinner and experiences betrayal and chaos. His heart never rests nor beats a soothing rhythmic pattern. Every night in the darkness of his bedroom Billy sits until the early hours of the morning in a red, oversized chair: besieged.

Exhausted, he sleeps as the last resort. It is almost dawn.

And yet, Billy's spirit flourishes. His love of life vibrates with an almighty strength that is like a spiritual current that flows within him. In that moment Billy's shell-shocked body is not a finite reality determined by science. No, the transcendent uplifts his spirit and tenderly Jesus is calling to him and me to "come home". In the narrow bathroom, Billy sits on the white toilet seat and praises the lord. His head slightly cocked, he swaggers gently. His torso, arms, and legs move effortlessly as he closes his eyes and smiles, face lifted to the sky. And then it happens. His light is so bright that for a split moment his ailing body levitates to a crescendo of resounding peace.

Little Rip Currents
October 2010

Once a month I drive into Boston to attend a two-hour meeting at Mass General Hospital. The Family Advisory Council is a group of doctors, nurses, administrators, and parents who address how to better integrate a family-centered care model into the daily realities of hospital protocols. Parents participate in and collaborate with medical personnel on committees that cover the "delivery of care; policy program development and evaluation; health care facility design; and professional education." It is an effective way to incorporate and reinforce the value of the family and patient perspectives.

But these monthly round-table discussions also serve as a powerful reminder of the need for compassion. That Tuesday night in the fall, the topic of closure in the midst of grief is discussed. Some of the parents on the council have children who have undergone multiple surgeries. Some of the parents have children whose health issues are acute and chronic. Some parents have children whose quality of life is vastly improved as a result of hospital care. Some parents have children who died in their efforts to save them. As a participant, I listen and learn from those parents who struggle to understand how they and their families are impacted. As the discussion concludes, a parent whose child had died looks at me across the table and says, "Well in your case there must be a stream of grieving."

Taken aback by her candor, I reply, "Yes, that is true in part," and say no more. I am overwhelmed by her wisdom. It is so rare to hear someone articulate my sensations of grief. Grief leads to closure but is also a wayward stream that flows in and out of my life, Billy's life, our life.

That evening I drive home and remember. Remembering cannot change what happened. Almost twenty-one years later, I know that rip currents of grief surface. My resurfaced grief throws me off guard. Years of experience cannot shelter my psyche from the undercurrent. Bill and Ashley's wedding presented a rip current that I did not see coming.

I am elated that the entire family will congregate and celebrate the wedding at the Cape. Billy will be able to attend because we can drive to our Cape Cod home. He will have a familiar home base and the wedding festivities will be at a boathouse on the beach. My expectations rise. We have flexible options. Billy can go and stay as long as he wants and return to the home base. This is Billy's first wedding. My central question is: What will Billy wear? This is fun. I consult with my son Ben about what is 20s hip. I carefully pack Billy's clothes in a separate suitcase. I want Billy to be with us that night at the boathouse in Chatham. His brand-new J-Crew camel corduroy blazer, blue-tones checked, collared shirt paired with a narrow, striped two-tone blue tie lie strewn over a chair in our bedroom. He never gets to wear his new finery. He never experiences my brother's and Ashley's wedding at a boathouse on the ocean. He never hears the bagpiper's music soar through the rising mist, the ever-changing cloud patterns, and the gentle rippling of the wild sea grass on the dunes. He never dances, laughs, and marvels at Bill and Ashley's sultry wedding dance.

It comes down to the wire. The readings, the vows and the cocktail hour pass. Matt makes the final call on his cell phone to find out how Billy is doing. Billy is in pain. It isn't the autism that thwarts a dream. It is autism and pain. Matt relays to me the answer. I nod. Our hearts ache with pangs of grief.

Bill comes over and asks me if Billy is coming. I tell him that we don't think so but that he has requested cake. Bill immediately goes to the kitchen and returns with multiple servings of a wedding cake that is adorned with two Adirondack chairs on the top tier. I thank him. We hug. And I tuck the bag under the cloth-covered table.

A wayward stream, a wedding steeped in devotion, our river moves on . . .

Dairy Free

Billy will never tolerate the allergy tests that could pinpoint the source of his constant throat discomfort. An allergist informs Matt and me that the only way to determine the cause is to eliminate all suspected food allergens. Dairy, egg, and gluten-free must be the baseline. In her professional opinion, it is not optional.

I don't, however, want to tell Billy. I don't want it to be true. I don't want to deliver the message that his horizon is about to shrink even further. Twenty-one years of going out to restaurants on the weekends or ordering take-out just ceases to exist? I cannot be a part of this cruel scenario. Restaurant review with Billy is a quintessential social happening. The elaborate and diverse menu of restaurant logos on his device combined with an infinite array of specific cuisine choices is one of his greatest indulgences. Billy has the freedom to choose because his device is programmed with specific commercial venues. Gleefully and on the verge of giddy, Billy peruses, angsts, and occasionally presses the Speaking Dynamically Pro button that generates a male voice that says in no uncertain terms "I changed my mind." With satisfaction that he can be the discussion leader, Billy returns swiftly to the restaurant page. Thursday night is Billy's pre-game party. The salivary glands piqued, Billy scans his options like a restaurant critic pondering every minutia of the dining experience.

I cannot, however, will away the night after night of massive throat throttles that plague him into the early morning hours. Billy hardly sleeps. Like an old man, he sits straight up in his overstuffed red chair and circulates incessantly the saliva he cannot swallow. Billy's esophagus is allergic to the very food groups I thought sustained him. Most young men welcome, relish, and search incessantly for the opportunity to eat any display of food. Like his fellow food enthusiasts, Billy intensely desires food. But after most meals his esophagus spasms in response to what his body registers as a hostile intruder. His digestive system under attack, Billy roars. The searing pain overwhelms him. As if the enemy is in close pursuit, he seeks cover. Billy runs the hallway, screams electric bolts, and pounds thunderously the top of his head. There is no answer.

There is no refuge. No matter what extreme physical retaliation he tries, he cannot extricate these foreign bodily sensations. The spasms end when the allergic reaction subsides. I can no longer eat dinner in the kitchen with Billy. The pending hailstorms of pain diminish my desire or enjoyment of food. Billy agrees. Every night, he anxiously anticipates what will happen to him at dinner. He doesn't understand the terminology of eosinophilic esophagitis. It is not necessary. He experiences the intricacies of this diagnosis every night. His anticipation of pain at dinner stresses his central nervous system uncontrollably. Moans of pain echo down the hallway as he showers before dinner each night. Dinner is subterfuge. Billy knows the risks involved. We all do.

The device is placed on the white Formica kitchen counter. Matt and Billy stand side by side as they do every Thursday night. The device is the language and Matt is the appointed messenger. Using the device, Billy's language system, Matt explains to Billy why he can no longer go to or order from restaurants. The explanation is simple and clear. The male voice output says, "Billy, the food gives you pain." The symbol shows a stomach with black lines darting out in every direction. It suggests a stomach in chaos. The alternative presented by Matt is that they will instead "cook meals at home." It is not a tantalizing alternative. Diplomatically, Billy objects and reiterates on the device that he wants to go to a specified restaurant. But his protest is not fierce. It lacks the firebrand rebuttal that is his signature trademark. Several times Billy challenges the statement but the tone is muted and then he just ends the discussion. Billy is not stressed. He is relieved. He no longer shoulders the burden alone. It is no longer a personal hell that becomes an embarrassing public event every time he finishes a meal.

The next weekend is the true test. Saturday morning Matt brings out the oversized blue thermal lunchbox and asks Billy what he'd like to pack. As if he had done this all his life, Billy rummages through the freezer and cabinets and hand picks all his lunch items. Billy is meticulous. That afternoon in the parking lot adjacent to an Audubon trail, Billy and Matt sit in the car and eat their respective gluten and dairy-free lunches. There is no anticipation of going to a selected restaurant. There is no ambient music. There is no young waitress eager to please. There is no perusing of the menu. There is no people watching. There is no opportunity to order one's favorite soda. Billy and Matt's dining experience amounts to social isolation. "Substantially separate" is the special-education term that historically describes Billy's educational environment. It's a lonely place.

That Saturday afternoon, Matt and I are the students and Billy is our esteemed teacher. The Diagnostic and Statistical Manual of Mental Disorders, or what is commonly referred to as DSM IV, includes a detailed list of the early signs that define autism. Desire for "sameness" leading to a resistance to change is highlighted as well as a lack of "intuitive social understanding." That Saturday afternoon, Billy's actions defy the strict categories outlined by the DSM IV. Billy intuitively understands that he must forgo the comfort of his familiar routine. The communication is crystal clear. Billy knows that Matt loves and respects him. He eats his lunch in the car because he understands the reasons why, and he knows his dad will be by his side. The definition of autism is complex and should be immediately followed by a disclaimer that states, "Although autism is complex disorder, no one can predict what the potential outcomes will be. No one."

And then every hurting parent should know about Billy and Matt's weekend excursions with a packed lunch in a blue thermal lunch bag.

The Manger

This is our first Christmas shared together as a nuclear family. Ben is twenty four and Billy is twenty one.

Christmas morning this year, Matt, Ben, and I fix our coffees with the requisite half and half and light sugar packets and meander into the family room off the kitchen. We are in no rush. Christmas lasts all day and night. We sip our Starbucks Christmas brew and luxuriate in our familiar surroundings. Wrapped in a purple throw and seated cross-legged in the middle of the sofa, Ben is content to just sip his coffee. Matt and I feel the same and settle into oversized chairs that frame Ben in an oval configuration. Quietly, we wait. We aren't sure what will happen. There is no predetermined protocol. We do not discuss whether Billy will participate. That line of thinking is foreign and irrelevant. Instead, we anticipate his arrival. There is no pretense. It is just understood that we want to wish him a Merry Christmas. With inexplicable timing, Billy slips into the kitchen and spies us straight ahead congregated next to the floor to ceiling, shimmering Christmas tree.

Ben's motion is subtle and would have been easily missed amongst the crazed chaos of our typical Christmas gatherings in Ohio. Ben says nothing. He smiles at Billy who lingers on the step that leads to us and then taps the cushion next to him. On the exact spot where Ben's hand brushes the upholstery, Billy joins Ben. Ben and Billy connect in this moment in anticipation of opening their gifts as brothers. In twenty-one years, this gathering has never happened. As Matt distributes the gifts, Ben and Billy never move. The sides of their bodies lightly brush each other. With all the gifts now arranged in four messy piles, Billy grabs a gift, unwraps it, and reaches for the next one. With forbearance and grace, Ben communicates with Billy. He places his hand on his chest and asks Billy to wait because it is his turn. Billy nods and hurriedly waves his hands up and down signaling that he knows and he will, but that it is taxing. Staircase landings lead somewhere. It is the years of Christmas landings, steps, and family that bestow upon us this current view of Billy and Ben together on Christmas morning.

Massillon Humor Winter 2011

Groggy, with my eyelids lowered somewhere in the white china mug, I am engrossed in my first morning cup of coffee. Billy is at the opened refrigerator door surveying his bounty. We are not synchronized. He is chipper. I am not. Late nights are his forte. Throat clearing at two in the morning never dampens Billy's fighting spirit.

Today is the next day, and he is game for a little fun. This is what I call "Massillon" humor. With the refrigerator whipped wide open, Billy picks up the pint of organic Vermont half and half, turns around, points to the little carton, beams, and vocalizes a question sound. Aroused out of my coffee stupor, I immediately object and tell Billy that he cannot have that dairy product. I repeat the party line: "Billy, the dairy will give you pain in your stomach."

Acting like he isn't sure he got the message, Billy holds up the refrigerator contraband, grins, and reiterates his question. All riled up, I start to protest and then I realize that I've just been conned. The bluff worked. Billy got a rise out of me. Satisfied and tickled pink, Billy returns the cream to its rightful place, shuts the door hard, and goes about his business. There is no doubt that Billy is a direct descendent of his Great Grandpa Bill, who hailed from Massillon, Ohio. Like his Grandpa, Billy inherently knows that a prank and a hearty chuckle is the bread of life. Dairy-free be damned!

I'm Not Sorry

It's 9 a.m. Billy is in the bathroom brushing his teeth. I'm in the kitchen on the phone, attending to a domestic matter. Multitasking. I hear Billy's baritone rumble in the background. I know that Holly is with him and she will assist. But in a split second I see Billy streak down the hall past the kitchen through my peripheral vision.

When the pain surfaces for Billy, he runs the hallways like a track star on steroids. Howls of distress permeate the air. In our house, it has become almost mundane. Our new normal. I keep talking to the guy on the other end of the phone as if the backdrop is pleasant white noise. Billy's predictable pain trip is to run the two adjoining hallways, then jump hard and fast in precise places on the runners. But he makes an unexpected detour. In order to muffle the noise, I twist my body away from the commotion while cradling the phone in a slightly bent-over position.

Pain enters the kitchen. It is not Billy. But it is Billy who clobbers me over the head and races away as if pursued by some unseen ominous entity. I'm rattled. I'm embarrassed. I'm not hurt. Without a glitch I politely wrap up the phone call. The phone call is complete. The task is accomplished. I got through it. But I'm not through it.

Facing the mirror, Billy is back in the bathroom. Repeatedly and wildly rubbing his hands through his hair, he works furiously to suppress the pain impulses that travel the length of his twenty-one-year-old body. I stand in the archway of the bathroom door. His pain is no longer my immediate concern. I want emotional recompense. I want the unexpected to cease.

Billy looks at me. His facial expression is etched in anxiety. Billy also wants the unexpected to cease. Neither one of us registers each other. The son and mother are not present. With venom in my tone, I tell Billy that he must say he is "sorry" for what he did. The word "sorry" ignites Billy's wrath. He hits me again. But I don't care. I seek an admission of guilt. Defiant, Billy stands his ground. There is no confession. There is only sorrow in the bathroom. I back down. I am baffled by Billy's strident "no" to hearing the word "sorry". Perhaps Billy is right. There is no blame to be cast. Billy and I struggle with our sorrow. That's enough.

Cracks

Billy's hands are weathered. The skin on his fingers and palms is drawn and callous. His hands lack a supple quality that youth imparts. Fissures wrap like a cord around each thumb. The skin beneath is smooth and vulnerable to infection. At the base of each finger, the skin splinters into deep lines. His own skin is not protecting him.

The dermatologist suggests a twice-daily application of Aquaphor ointment to fend off further deterioration. When the splits widen, a prescription is used to ward off bleeding and infection. Billy's immune system seems lacking. His physical system will not self-correct. He has always had eczema issues. With time and treatment, however, these skin flare-ups used to resolve. Not anymore. The autoimmune switch is not fully powered.

I'm Not Invisible
July 2011

B illy is out of the house. It has become a rare occurrence. But on this hot, sunny July day, Billy is pumped to be out of the house and on the road. On the car ride to Hannah's yoga studio, Billy rocks out to the latest club hits. A change of pace and a new venue for practice is a welcome antidote. Saddled with his device and another case filled with yoga paraphernalia, Billy runs up the office stairs and on the final stair ascent, he trips forward. His wrist slams down hard on the bare cement step as the straps and bags slump heavily over his shoulders. Bleeding slightly from a cut on the inside of his wrist and wincing from the jarring impact, he is livid. Years of chronic pain have taken their toll. Patient surrender is not in his vocabulary. His physical experience of any pain, accidental or otherwise, now triggers a lightening response of fight. His central nervous system is primed for war: Billy yells, jumps, and runs frantically back and forth in front of the contemporary and cleanly designed reception area. This whisper-quiet air-conditioned waiting area is now alit with adrenaline as Billy copes and sideswipes anything in his path. One more mishap. One more setback.

Fighting back the tears from his embarrassing display of human chaos, Billy regroups, picks up his bags, and plows his way down the softly lit hallway. Entering Hannah's yoga studio, he abruptly discards his bags on the floor in a tangled heap. Distressed and sweating, he paces all four corners of Hannah's yoga studio. In this sanctuary, Billy seeks atonement and closure for his public outburst. Physical and emotional recovery is grueling work. The self-imposed rituals expel all remnants of negative energy. It is an exhausting but meaningful exorcism. Never coming up for breath, Billy chugs a bottle of strawberry-kiwi vitamin water. Pacing the length and width of the room, Billy pauses every few seconds and jumps. Leaning from the waist with his face parallel to the floor, he jumps in place with such force one can imagine the floor imprinted with his black, high-top Nikes. Energy oozes from every tilt, step, and breath.

In precision form, Billy takes a few steps forward and halts as he races his calloused dry hands through his hair. Beaded in sweat, he monitors others' movements as he struggles to reset. No sudden changes. No new information. This is his path toward levity. As Billy's chest heaves gradually slow down, his clipped breathing elongates. A commanding Billy now stands in the middle of the room. His eyes dart back and forth as he scans the premises.

A door at the far side of the room opens and a tall young man with his head slightly bowed walks quickly past Billy. Billy observes him but the young man does not make eye contact. The young man returns and walks again right past Billy into the adjacent filing room. Alert and now focused, Billy monitors the young man's every return move. Unperturbed and without hesitation, Billy picks up his device, accesses his "Friends" page and follows the young man into the cramped filing quarters. Billy chooses to stand eye to eye with the young man as he points and presses the question, "Who are you?" Billy delivers direct eye contact. Curious, he waits politely for an answer.

Billy shakes the young man's hand because it is the natural thing to do.

Beseech - July 2011

Chronic pain creeps steadily and in unexpected designs. Billy knows this. He tries hard every hour of every day to keep the pain underground. He wants to move on. Determination alone, however, will not squelch his bodily dysfunctions. Adrenaline rushes occur daily. After any physical activity, his eyes dilate and sweat drips from every pore. Frustrated, Billy grabs towels to douse the sweat from his hair and forehead. He lifts his t-shirt and wipes his armpits. He can't stand the profuse sweat. It's intrusive and irritating. It's been just weeks since a massive rash surrounding each of his armpits required medical attention. Billy is always in flux. Inflammation radiates from his body. With his upper torso tilted downward, he jumps in frenzied bursts. His landings pound the ground as he searches for distractions from his own body's fiery pulsations. A bright red flush combs his limbs, face, and torso. Billy manages the pain eruptions as best he can. Matt and I tell ourselves that Billy's health has improved. That conclusion blurs our vision. From our vantage point, Billy's pain is fleeting. Except that the fleeting outbursts occur daily.

Billy's post-yoga routine is usually seamless. When yoga is finished, Billy, Hannah, and Shelley return from the barn and enter Billy's art studio in the garage. Sitting on the bench, he takes off his shoes and enters home school. At some point in transition, Billy grabs a snack, slurps a popsicle, or downs a carbonated beverage. The routine is consistent, clear and ordinary. It is conflict free.

But not on this summer day.

Muffling the moan utterances, Billy runs from the barn to the house. Yoga session is complete. As he enters the garage art studio and walks through to home school, pain flashes.

I am upstairs in the kitchen and I hear physical commotion and shouts of "No Billy! No!" Alarmed, I run downstairs. Billy is enraged. I command Shelly and Hannah to keep their distance. They move quickly into the adjacent garage and stand next to the backdoor. Julia, Billy's art teacher, waits behind the locked door in home school. Exits secured. No one is truly safe, however, including Billy. I approach Billy. I don't speak, and I don't see it coming.

With lightning speed, Billy's open hand forcefully hits bulls-eye the left side of my face. Reeling, I turn away and yell. My eye area swelling, I move into the outer basement in an effort to avoid Billy's fury. I unlock the basement door, run up to the kitchen, and fill a Ziploc bag with ice. I run back downstairs, lock the home-school door and wait. I'm in the outer basement. My eye area pulsates. Pressing the ad-hoc ice pack to my eye, I do not stir. I do not make eye contact. I do not speak. Billy does not look like himself. I cannot detect Billy. His adrenaline overpowers his senses. There is no skid brake. He is a moving swath of unbridled energy. Back and forth, he rants, raves, paces, jumps hard, and screams with his muscled arms flapping like wings behind his head. His face is crimson. His facial features recede into the sockets and cavities. Billy and I are stuck in a place where neither of us wants to be. The manic pacing slows as he rubs his hands through his hair. Still sweating, Billy wipes forcefully his forehead with his shirtsleeve. Audibly breathing, Billy comes over and gently touches the ice bag and looks at me inquisitively. Billy notices. I say nothing. I stand and wait. I am his guardian. Sitting down on the red bench, he wipes his brow again, bows his head and stares with eyes wide open at his shoes. His physical motions are no longer in overdrive. Silently tears release.

"I think it's the paints." That's what Julia says to me.

Holding an ice-filled Ziploc bag to my left eye I ask, "Billy, what paints do you want?"

Deftly, he maneuvers to the art page and then to the colors page and answers on his device, "Blue, gold and green."

Julia, his art teacher, gives him back the clear plastic receptacles that contain each of the colors Billy noted. He places them back in the milk container with the pile of paint receptacles. He walks back into home school and sits down on his favorite tangerine, armless chair. Kneeling in front of Billy, I watch him. He gestures toward my bag-covered eye, and I tell him that, "It must stay." The damage is real. I place my hand on his leg and Billy bends slightly forward, pauses and beseeches me. His aqua blue eyes are riveted to mine. He never blinks. I am awash in forgiveness. I did not expect to feel somber and grateful.

Part Five:
Recovery

After years of crisis and medical trial and error, Billy slowly reclaims his life. Deep sadness, anger, insecurity, and fear are gradually replaced by a holistic self- awareness and maturity. Billy faces his body's limitations, and begins to express himself in surprising and creative ways.

This Little Light of Mine

As Billy's illness mushrooms in diverse medical directions, I am consumed by the flurry of doctors' visits, medical procedures, emergencies, drug trials, and setbacks. Every ounce of my kinetic energy is devoted to caring for and observing Billy twenty-four hours a day. This is a high alert. The doctors need data points. The more pain Billy endures, the less desire he has to communicate. Topics concerning pain and emotions are highly charged with anxiety, guilt, and uncertainty about how to interpret these raw sensations. Part of his coping mechanism is to burrow under pillows and heavy blankets. Billy cannot comment on or answer questions about his body. Pointing is too difficult. Documenting every expression no matter how subtle requires vigilant observation. Anyone who participates in home school or helps take care of Billy is recruited. They form a volunteer corps. We film. We record in medical logs. We research medical resources online for any clue, clarification, or new avenues to ponder. We share anecdotes in the hallway and outside the bathroom. Anywhere. We reconvene and review the information over and over. Anywhere. Our home is a domestic version of a live ER, and House, M.D. wrapped into one.

By most outsiders' accounts, the situation is chaotic, grim, and probably unsustainable. And yet in the midst of this chaos, there is something else emerging in our domicile. At first it is barely a glimmer in the overstuffed and dimly lit outer basement. It could easily have been overlooked. Hoisting the Whole Food bags on both shoulders to avoid multiple trips, I scurry into the outer basement. Overloaded and slightly bent over, I head straight to the door that leads up to the kitchen; I sense a kaleidoscope of colors in my peripheral vision. Lifting my body straight up through the weighted baggage, I stop, drop my bags, and breathe in the effervescent colors traversing the white canvas. Punches of neon pink. Arcs of lime green. Loops of deep red and flicks and scoops of cobalt blue. Color and texture abound in the windowless outer basement where Billy experiments.

The opportunity to paint might not have happened. Teachers of students on the autism spectrum do not view their students as creative expressionists. When he was a young child, I brought to the classroom the paints and materials so that Billy could play with colors. At the time it was a hunch. Now I am a captive audience of one. Almost every night I pause and take notice as if I'm at the Museum of Fine Arts, standing mesmerized by a larger-than-life, floor-to-ceiling work of Rothko or Pollack. It is a nightly ritual. As one winter season replaces another, the motions intensify. Flicks and broad strokes collide in space. Colors that I never imagined intertwine and evolve into dynamic swaths. Awestruck, I respond. As if Billy and I signed a secret pact, I search for tools. I venture to hardware stores, automotive shops, paint stores, pharmacies, and every "kitchen" department within a twenty-mile radius. Often I buy in duplicates so that Billy can use both of his hands to whirl paint however he chooses. Cashiers often question my intentions and depending on my state of mind, I tell them that my son Billy and I are artists. Most times, I receive respectful, even enthusiastic nods of approval. Billy and I are on a quest to tap into and unleash our delight in color and movement. Our ambitions are instinctive. Primordial. Our collaboration is intuitive. Nothing is ever said. Nothing is analyzed. In the subterranean basement removed from all the pain, anxiety, and medical terminology, Billy radiates light.

When I think about how in the midst of his darkest moments, Billy painted, I am reminded of a gospel song that I sang as a child. "This Little Light of Mine" was a personal favorite. I remember singing the lyrics at the top of my lungs as my hands formed a light that I knew would never be extinguished. A child's faith, and I daresay our faith, lives in the basement. The burning embers glow bright. "This little light of mine, I'm going to let it shine. Let it shine. Let it shine, all the time."

Monday Night Huddle
September 2011

Matt and I huddle with Billy's original neurologist, Dr. Bauman, around a small screen ready to videoconference with the Autism Think Tank. After years of brainstorming and procedures, Dr. Buie, Billy's gastroenterologist, has recommended that we confer with this consortium of doctors from diverse medical disciplines who specialize in complex cases. As a member of the Autism Think Tank, Dr. Buie is prepared to lead the discussion.

The computer screen of the live feed shows a nondescript conference room with some individuals filtering in. No one seems prepared to begin. The sound is muffled and not all the specialists at other locations are online or in their respective offices. The office that we are in is small and sterile. The airflow is low. Multiple AV problems delay the start time. I'm not sure we will get connected to all the parties involved. After thirty minutes of "Can you hear me now?" Dr. Buie begins the meeting by having each of the participants introduce themselves. Matt outlines Billy's medical history and current challenges. We describe at length Billy's daily adrenaline swings and the pain that follows. One of the lead members of the team is a psychiatrist who for forty years was involved in state-run mental-health institutions in Ohio. He is situated in his home office in a small town near Columbus, Ohio. The sound is at times distorted and the doctor is physically awkward and somewhat unfamiliar with the technology. His thoughts, however, are lucid. He has clearly reviewed the medical intricacies of Billy's ongoing ordeal. Serious and pointed in his remarks, there is a sense of urgency and compassion for Billy's medical realities. The audio is patchy as we strain to hear and understand the basis for his recommendations.

Parasympathetic and sympathetic systems are out of sync. Billy's autonomic nervous system doesn't regulate properly. Adrenaline breaks through the brain blood barrier and what ensues is what is referred to as an "autonomic storm". In other words, Billy's pain receptors are on constant high alert and any perceived disruption causes him to escalate. Even minor altercations such as bumping his leg against a table can cause an extreme response. Eyes dilated, Billy sweats profusely and breathes at a rapid pace. Wildly jumping and screaming, Billy is in chaos. His sympathetic system accelerates out of control. The doctor believes that Billy's actions demonstrate a need for a beta-blocker that will slow down the autonomic response. The beta-blocker will engender a calming effect that will diminish the acceleration of the adrenaline response.

The underground parking lot is deserted at 10 o'clock on Monday night. Matt and I thank Dr. Bauman for attending the meeting. The information is overwhelming. Another medical issue to add to Billy's plate and another medication to assess. By the time we review the information with Billy's doctors it will be the end of October. There are no guarantees. None of our doctors have direct experience with such a tactic. It is a trial-and-error approach. The process, in terms of delivery of the medication, will be incremental. It is another maybe.

As Billy's extreme reactions to minor disruptions become more measured, he notices and enjoys the presence of others. It is a turning point.

Panoramic

It's Billy third try. It's not his fault. There is no information or coaching that will stop an automatic reflex. Billy is 21 years old. He braces his chin into the plastic receptacle and moves closer to the cold interior of the panoramic X-ray apparatus. Patiently he waits for the dental assistant to push the button and signal the green light. Determined to let the camera take the angles, Billy grips down and stands straight and still. Just on the verge of a successful shoot, the camera angles precipitously close to his face as it conducts it three-dimensional rotation of the jaw. His body reacts. It is a barely-discernible motion. It doesn't matter. The film is compromised and inadmissible as data. I inform Billy that we are done. He takes off the weighted vest, grabs the social story about the steps involved in participating in a panoramic X-ray, wads it into a ball and shoves it in the trash can. Humiliated, Billy leads the way out of the adult practice and barrels into the more congenial pediatric office. Billy knows the turf. Almost everyone there has known Billy since he was a preschooler. Pushing the double doors open, he heads straight to the balloon counter. In no uncertain terms, he demands that someone blow up the balloon. Always receptive to Billy's requests, he is given a red balloon on a short string. He turns 360 degrees and walks out of the building with Holly and I following his lead. Now in the back parking lot, Billy crams his balloon into a dumpster, pitches his bag into the car, gets in and slams the backseat door.

Now we have no choice but to get the wisdom teeth X-rays under general anesthesia. I am more depressed that Billy feels like he failed.

Whole Foods Betrayal
October 2011

There are a host of possible explanations as to why Billy initiates a brawl in the dental office at MGH. Before our departure, we show Billy a photo of the main MGH entrance. Technically, we are going to an adjacent building. Maybe that lit the fuse. We do not drive into the garage parking lot. Instead we enter at a parking lot that is located above ground and surrounded by stores. As we "turn the wrong way," Billy's radar is activated. Sitting in the back seat, his body moves forward and his head turns in a different direction. Tension permeates his increasingly loud intonations. Billy doesn't know the premises. His disapproval mounts as we secure a parking spot. The lot is packed. There is hardly any space to open the car door and squeeze out. A well-dressed older woman expresses audible disapproval as Billy jumps and sweats on the black pavement at the rear of the car. Billy is wired. I'm on high alert but I am hoping Billy will be okay once he sees that it's just another doctor's office visit. As we try to expedite our short trip into the building, I see out of my peripheral vision the Whole Foods store. In the same instant I see Billy focus on the window display that is chock full of sweets. A shadow crosses Billy's face as his lips form a sneer. Betrayed and now denied, we are entering the perfect storm.

Matt, Billy, Holly, and I enter the elevator. Everyone is silent and coiled. Billy seethes. As the elevator doors open, Billy rushes out, jumps and hollers. I tell Matt to take him to the restroom while I try to convince the receptionist to put us in an office right away. I sense the need to contain. The assistant accesses Billy's record. As I lean against the half-wall, time warps. Moments seem like an eternity. Hearing the ruckus as Billy and Matt enter the reception area, the front desk expedites the paperwork and finds a space down the hallway in the far right corner. I breathe hard as we congregate in the dentist's office. I smile at the assistant as she reassures us that the dentist will be in momentarily. I am just relieved that the door is shut.

No one can contain an autonomic storm. Maybe it was the fact that the room contained a dental chair and instruments. From Billy's perspective, it didn't look like an office meeting space. I will never know for certain. Without warning, Billy levels his open hand as hard as he can across Matt's face. Matt's glasses fly as he stumbles back. The left side of his nose is red and swelling. The dentist knocks on the door. I look at the situation, open the door slightly, and request that Billy needs a little time to adjust. We all do.

Waiting Room Protocol
December 2011

Billy is in good spirits as we enter the gastrointestinal unit. In previous visits, Billy was too sick to notice other people. Right at this moment Billy is curious as he scans all the people sitting in the reception room. Intrigued, Billy navigates on his device to the dictionary page and then to the doctors page. As we try to walk straight ahead, Billy leans left. Matt and I try to redirect Billy but he will not be denied. He gently approaches a woman, leans down, smiles, presses the button that speaks in a Siri-like voice, "Who are you?" Pointing to the various doctors' faces and names on the page, Billy infers that she must be a doctor. He believes that only doctors inhabit the hospital. No longer in a pain-induced fog, Billy emerges. Autism remains, however, and now I need to teach Billy the meaning of the word patient. Patients have never been part of Billy's working vocabulary, only doctors.

Everybody Be Quiet
December 2011

B illy has just been wheeled into the waiting room directly across from the operating room. With Herculean effort on Matt's part, we have assembled doctors across disciplines to examine and treat Billy. First, the gastrointestinal specialist will conduct an upper endoscopy to evaluate the level of deterioration. Then the dental team will take X-rays to identify the rate of growth and positioning of his wisdom teeth. Eight cavities will be filled and teeth will be cleaned. All of these procedures will proceed under only one administration of anesthesia.

It is an indistinct space except for the single window that looks out on some green corridor space engulfed by the looming hospital infrastructure. The December sky is electric blue and the sunshine filters in through the single window. No one seems to notice except Billy. Sporting a 24-hour blond-red beard and wearing a body-snug Vince t-shirt with biceps to match, he actually looks quite hip. Smiling, Billy peers out the window. He is the calmest and definitely the coolest in this crowd. The pre-op nurse, the operating-room nurse, the anesthesiologist, the dentist, and the gastrointestinal specialist have all filed in. They disseminate information, ask questions, present the legal forms, and wait for the required guardian signatures. They are polite, respectful, but tense. Billy is certainly not giving them any reason for heightened anxiety. He greets every medical professional with an open handshake, direct eye contact, and a slight devilish grin. Billy knows the drill and appears calm, cool, and collected. The prevailing viewpoint, however, is that a nonverbal young man with autism cannot maintain his composure in this crisis-oriented environment. The anesthesiologist re-enters the room and asks Matt and I again whether Billy needs a sedative before going into the operating room. We reiterate no. We tell the conscientious doctor that all Billy needs is a precise and expedited execution of the plan. Have the needle ready to go and I will count until Billy is under. It is a foolproof drill.

We are confident. Billy is confident. Just tell us when and we will roll Billy in. Dressed in blue scrubs but no blue hats (per request of Billy), Matt and I stand on each side of Billy's gurney. We've got the green light. As the double doors swing open and the fluorescent operating lights highlight the area, I hear noise. It's not the momentum of a battle-tested procedure. What I hear is talk. Elevated inquiry. Adrenaline-surged commentary. Delay. So I blink, raise my hands, and announce to the preeminent medical staff and faculty, "Everybody, be quiet!"

The sounds cease. Billy focuses on my counting. That's all it takes. Silence.

Blueberry Muffins
December 2011

Billy's mouth contorts diagonally, sideways, and up and down. Sitting upright on a gurney in post-op, he circumnavigates every angle of his mouth cavity. His eyes roll up into his head as he delays the inevitable gulp. After two hours with a tube down his throat for an endoscopy and dental work, blueberry muffins are borderline torturous to swallow. But there is no stopping Billy even if he whimpers as he grinds, gnashes, and gulps hard, morsel by morsel. We made a deal. "First shot, endoscopy, dental work, and then two fat muffins." That's what I put in writing and that's what I confirmed via the customized pages on his Toughbook laptop. Billy is a tough negotiator and a deal is a deal. I could tear up the paper in pieces and discard the written version, but the Toughbook pages are non-negotiable. Furthermore, my stated promise secures Billy's trust now and in the future. Groggy but in charge, Billy will not be denied his treat. He met his end of the bargain. I offer him the Mott apple juice can as a possible substitute. Immediately, Billy dismisses my suggestion. I counter and propose that maybe just one large blueberry muffin will suffice. No way. First we have the two blueberry muffins. That's the relevant detail. My stress mounts as I witness Billy shove an enormous piece into his mouth. His eyes roll again as he swallows through an arid and sore esophagus. I have only one card left and I play it. Standing next to his hospital bed, I count like a catcher giving signals to the pitcher. Each slow count of ten delays Billy's effort to eat the muffins like a fast-food item. The visual of my fingers counting in a rhythmic motion before he tears off each bite is tolerated as an acceptable compromise. The visuals always clarify the situation. So we hold a 30-minute vigil while Billy consumes two large blueberry muffins bought as a reward from the MGH cafe. Matt, Holly, the attending nurse, and I can only squirm and wince as Billy reclaims his right to eat blueberry muffins in the recovery room. Every prior hospital procedure included a post-op muffin. The hospital routine trumps Billy's personal comfort.

Art and Charisma
2011 to 2012

Billy loves going to a community art studio located in a warehouse near the Tufts University campus. The space is drafty, gritty, and unorganized. The heating and cooling system is erratic. The noise from the blowers is either deafening or dead silent. But that's irrelevant. This is the only quasi-social place that Billy ventures to outside his home. His health is precarious and how he feels at any given moment is unpredictable. Billy is passionate about painting as well as his new artist friends. Every Monday for a precious hour and a half, he begins his art session by sauntering into this space with confidence. Billy is the consummate politician. He takes out his device from his cool pouch bag that sports a few swatches of paint and approaches each individual along the way. With laser-sharp focus, Billy extends his open hand. Once contact is made, Billy greets them with a "Hi" he presses on his device. If their names and pictures have not been programmed, he turns immediately to me and points to the blank white cell indicating that I need to rectify the situation. I nod in agreement. Billy is his own man. Not deterred by those who seem less than pleased to be in this social entanglement, Billy smiles and moves on. Each ensuing week, Billy's support base grows. They sense his no-bullshit approach. The hardcore few that hold regular smoking sessions outside the metal door in the frigid cold are changing their tune. Billy is not only suave; he is sincere. The difference between Billy and the "politician" is that Billy doesn't harbor any ulterior motive. Every smile, direct eye contact, and strong handshake is authentic. There is nothing rote about it. More and more of his cohorts greet him by name or in one particular love-struck case yells across the warehouse, echoing the message, "I love you Billy!"

He is one of them as he sets up his schedules on the easel and changes into his work apron. There are so many high moments. During the winter, there are many Mondays that Billy listens to the great tenor, Pavarotti. One Monday a gentleman pulls up a chair so that he can join Billy in the celebration of art and music. In the far-reaching corner of a warehouse, Billy and his new friend revel with others artists working at neighboring tables. It is all so right.

Billy Wept

Billy wept. That's what Hannah and Jen told me when I arrived home from the grocery store on a January afternoon. In her new position as autism specialist, Holly had arranged for a peer from the JFCS program to join Billy in a yoga session. Billy is finally well enough to handle an orchestrated social engagement. I have no defined expectations. I cannot fathom, however, the outcome.

James and Billy meet for the first time in home school. Billy's eyes are focused exclusively on his teacher Jen as they negotiate the content and terms of his schedule for the day. A computerized shouting match requires Billy's undivided attention. James, clad in a navy blue parka with a faux-fur edged hood and wearing dark, oversized sunglasses, comes into home school to use the bathroom. Despite his uncanny peripheral vision, Billy doesn't notice James's arrival. An agreed-upon settlement reached, Billy heads to the bathroom. As he approaches the door, Billy is informed that he must wait until it is available. Within seconds, Billy sees James exit the bathroom. Without missing a beat, Billy runs to the table, grabs his device and like a man on a mission stands shoulder to shoulder with James. Looking directly at James, Billy swiftly navigates to the "Friends" page and presses the button that says, "What's your name?" James takes out of his coat pocket a small red communication book. He points to his name and the picture of Billy that Holly recently inserted. Billy shakes his hand. James gives Billy a high five. Their connection is spontaneous, as if they have always known each other.

James and Holly go out to the barn to wait for Billy while he completes the iPad segment of his master schedule. When Billy approaches the barn, he catches James's reflection as he butt jumps on the gymnastics standard trampoline. Billy smiles widely. With a light spring in his steps, he opens the dark green door with the four glass panels and hears James's familiar sounds. Billy and James share these primal yet personal sounds. James's voice arcs high and low and reverberates into the barn rafters. The barn reverberates the sound of unfettered joy. Billy sits down on the black wooden bench where he always takes off his shoes and socks. He does not, however, follow the autopilot routine.

Billy is not ready to join the others at yoga. Suddenly, Billy weeps. Tears stream down his face as he bows his head and cries softly. Unperturbed by Billy's sad continuous dirge, James waits for Billy to join him in their first yoga practice together led by Hannah, Billy's yoga teacher. It has been four years since Billy has been in the presence of his peers. The last time Billy saw his classmates was December 2007. Billy had just turned eighteen. Even then the "substantially separate" classroom setting discouraged social interaction. Individualized tasks were deemed more important. Billy is now twenty-two years old.

Perhaps Billy thought that he would never see a peer again.

Perhaps Billy felt that his years of illness and unrelenting pain would always be his only reality.

Perhaps Billy thought that his social world would only consist of caring older adults and a shrunken environment driven by medical emergencies and endless doctors' visits.

Perhaps Billy had stopped hoping.

Or maybe Billy in that moment realized that his life could change. His life could include friends.

Pulling himself together, Billy fights to regain his composure. Untying his sneakers that are tied compactly in a bow with knots that leave no spare lace, Billy leans over and places his sweat-soaked socks next to his shoes. He stands and moves toward James. It is time for yoga.

Billy initiates in a way that most human beings do not or cannot. Gently he holds James's hands and looks into his eyes. Unconditionally, Billy welcomes James.

The last yoga pose is shavasana. Billy and James lie down on their mats six inches away from each other. Weighted down by Navaho-style blankets that envelop their torsos, they open their arms and hands to the sky.

From years of practice, Billy understands the challenges as well as the abiding rest that stillness and breath gives him. James does not yet fully experience shavasana. It does not matter. Billy and James share blankets, space, and the gratitude of oneness. Billy's eyes are open.

My Communication Breakdown February 2012

A week to the day after meeting James for yoga, Billy heads out to the barn for his weekly yoga session with Hannah. Immersed in daily activities, I do not mention to Billy that James can't attend today. Nor do I mention the day or the week when he will return to yoga. I fail to communicate to the person who is directly impacted. It is my mistake.

Billy walks into the barn expecting James to be there. He is not. Billy sits down on the bench and cries. My heart aches knowing that I dashed Billy's hope.

There is no word for communication negligence. Just guilt.

Billy and James

It is the second yoga session that James has joined Billy at the barn. Excited to see James again, he smiles broadly at the news and immediately navigates on his device to the "Friends" page where James's photo is now posted.

In the sun-filled barn, Billy walks up to James and gently brushes his index finger on James's lower lip. Their eyes meet. James does not flinch. Billy waits. James articulates the sound that resonates, "Da." It is true. Billy confirms that he has a friend who is his peer. It is a first. It is time for their yoga session together.

New Hampshire Winter

I've been thinking about Billy's complex response to James's visit. I'm in Waterville, New Hampshire for the weekend. It's been four years to the month since I've been to our condo. The only reason I know this is because I pick up a pile of magazines on our bedside table and they are all dated 2008.

Living a triage lifestyle warps your sense of time. The last time I was here, it was Martin Luther King Jr.'s birthday in 2008. That Monday morning, Matt, Billy, and I headed for Crotched Mountain School. Billy had been working as an intern in the recycling department for the campus. I was so proud of him. He'd learned so many skills, followed multiple directions, and communicated independently on the work site. Billy was diligent and always professional. Matt had never seen Billy in this setting so we thought it would be a great opportunity to see Billy in action. No one in the schools had ever showcased Billy's strengths. There never was an open house. We'd never been invited to Billy's classroom to hear about upcoming curriculum. Matt and I savored Billy's accomplishments and like every other parent we wanted to cheer him on.

Before we ever got there, Billy showed signs of heightened distress. Sitting in the backseat of the car, Billy hit his head for almost two hours. At that moment we thought the transition from Waterville to Crotched Mountain was the problem. We'd always driven from home. This was a new route. Maybe Billy wasn't sure what was going to happen. Billy's anxiety mounted. The hitting became harder. No visual communication supports mattered. Once we arrived, empathetic support staff suggested that maybe the radio music was too loud or that maybe Billy had a sensory issue. Matt and I stood in the warehouse, unable to move. What we witnessed was utter dissolution. Billy stood at the crank where he took institutional-size food cans, placed them precisely under the lid remover, and turned the crank until the metal lid released. He threw the lids in a four-foot tall cardboard box. Without missing a beat, Billy then took the can and positioned it under his work boot and stomped it flat. Billy flung the scrap metal into another receptacle. After every can completion, Billy would walk over to us, look at us directly, take off his work gloves and with both hands hit the top of his head repeatedly. Matt and I couldn't bear to watch his self-injurious acts. We took Billy home. Heartbroken, shocked, and lost, neither Matt nor I could comprehend why Billy battered his own body.

Four years later, I am zipped up in my 15-year-old ski jumpsuit and layered from head to toe so that I can take a long winter walk in the White Mountain National Forest. Along the route I take in the view of the snow-dusted pines on the mountain. I pause and breathe in the cold, clean mountain air. I know where I'm going. I'm no longer lost. Taking a left past the Waterville Ski Academy, I trudge my way over the snow-packed road toward Mad River Creek. On the overpass, I stop to look at the ice-encrusted river.

The path to Waterville has had many detours along the way. As a preschooler, Billy's ski ventures were challenging. One weekend we were in Vermont for a ski adventure. The plan was that I would take Ben for his ski lessons and Matt would take Billy to a smaller mountain that hosted an adaptive ski program. At the end of the day, Ben and I returned to the condo. Invigorated by the mountain air, I was eager to find out how Billy's lesson went. Matt informed me that Billy never made it into the ski lodge. Billy stood at the entrance and screamed. My retort was that tomorrow Billy would get to the bench and try on his ski boots. Incredulous, Matt said out loud, "Go back?"

Several years later, Waterville Valley became our ski base. The Adaptive Ski program is housed in the main lodge. It is a community of skiers. One of the last times Billy ever skied with Matt, they were putting on their ski gear in the changing area. Some of the other fellows in the room were wounded soldiers from the Iraq War. Released from the Walter Reed Army Medical Hospital, they had traveled to Waterville to learn to ski without a body part. The room was crowded yet quiet. Billy gravitated toward one vet who had a new prosthetic leg. Overcome with natural curiosity, Billy reached his hand out, touched the young man's new leg and flashed him a one-hundred-watt smile. The intense expression on the soldier's face melted. He almost laughed. Billy's simple gesture lifted his spirit. The comfort level in the room increased tenfold.

After four years, however, my perspective is more diverse. In the forefront on the left side is a wide swath of hundreds of snow-tinged divots that pucker and float on the surface. Warmed by the sun, they appear like pale-green luminous crystals. The ice and snow cannot suppress the water flow. Right in the middle, there is a break in the river where the water flows freely and I see the interior view of stones and rocks lying still beneath the current. A short distance out are glistening white dollops of snow lightly mounted on the pulsating water beneath. In the distant background are birch trees resting horizontally across the waterway. And there is always the barely audible sound of water, wind, and motion. The winter scene dazzles with icy beauty. Barriers arise and the water flows another way. Backflow changes the physical design. In the midst of stillness, disruption and time, breakthroughs happen. Overall the scene brims with texture and purpose.

I'm so glad to understand the meaning of perspective.

No More Sunglasses

Billy once wore his hip, black Ray Bans or metallic silver Oakley shades all the time, but no longer. Morning, noon or night, the time of day was irrelevant. Seasonal fashion didn't matter. To the doctor's office, emergency room, hospital, or walking to the barn on a frozen winter night, those sunglasses were an appendage of his physical body.

Wearing sunglasses throughout his ordeal became a badge of sorrow and strength. His "warrior helmet" shielded him from the brutal and stark awareness that his life as he once knew it had dissolved. The protective plastic lenses tempered the harsh glare. Emotionally isolated with a physical body steeped in pain, he could stand tall, retreat, anguish, cry, and mourn with visually muted public scrutiny.

But then, Billy cuts the cord. It is not gradual. It is abrupt. It is decisive. Handing him his sunglasses for our trip to the doctor is customary. But not this day. He takes them and puts them back on the shelf.

"Billy, are you sure you don't want your sunglasses?" I ask. Without fanfare, Billy stands up, puts his coat, hat and gloves on. I ask again and he shakes his head "no." I look at Billy anew.

Billy's eyes reflect hues of blue and green. I had forgotten Billy's mischievous expression when he would grin. I'd forgotten how clear, focused, and engaged he could be. Billy rejects even the suggestion that he might need sunglasses. He no longer needs a screen. His vision is peripheral and forward-looking.

Yoga in Its Truest Form

Billy's yoga teacher Hannah has given me a draft of an article she is writing. Hannah writes the following:

> Throughout it all Billy and I continue to do our yoga. I adapted my sessions with Billy to accommodate his fluctuating needs. When he was too sick for vigorous practice, we did restorative poses with lots of props and long periods of relaxation. When the transition outside to the practice space in the barn became too difficult, we moved our mats into the house. When a terrible reaction to anti-seizure medication caused Billy to completely shut down, he could not make it onto the yoga mat at all. Just standing up would throw Billy into an onslaught of self-injurious behavior, causing more damage to his already bruised and bloodied face. Some of my sessions with Billy consisted of brief visits to his darkened bedroom. I wanted Billy to know I was there and still a part of his life. I quietly told Billy that I was sorry he was sick and I wanted him to feel better and get back to doing yoga soon. I'm not sure how many of those words Billy understood, but we made eye contact and he held my hand. That was yoga in its truest form.

I read this for the first time a few months ago. I did not witness their interaction. It doesn't matter. It isn't the point. I am grief stricken and thankful that this quiet, loving exchange occurred.

The road to recovery means that Billy believes that we love him no matter the circumstances and that all of us who care and work on Billy's behalf tell each other our stories. We all must cry. We all must heal.

A Japanese Maple
Spring 2012

A Japanese maple tree is planted in the garden bed in front of our house. This tree is distinctive even though it sits low to the ground. The trunk twists deeply, exposing the gnarled pathway. The spirals rivet the surface and leave coiled indentations. The wood is dense, solid, and worn. Last winter, we broke a snowfall record. The season was bitter and cold. Damage to trees was widespread. They could not withstand the pounding wind, ice, and heavy snow accumulations. Trees fell or lost limbs. That spring I noted that the trunk of our Japanese maple was almost severed. The split in the wood exposed the interior, forcing the limb to bow to the ground. The renowned feathery leaves were sallow in color, sapped of life. I was afraid that we'd lose this natural artistry.

This is the second spring after the record-breaking winter.

Atop this fractured base is now a cascade of feathery leaves. The delicate leaves cover sinewy branches. Burnished red foliage drapes, covers, and gravitates in all directions from the central stem. The vibrant energy and fragile nature of this tree endures. The damaged central artery did not fail.

This spring, Billy's health improves. The twists, turns, and contractions of his gastrointestinal system have abated. His esophagus is calmer. The violent throat clearing is diminished. Tremors, dizziness, and uncontrolled pain do not permeate every moment of his young life. The emotional whiplash of anger, depression, sadness, and remorse no longer consumes him. His burden is lighter.

The Billy who went AWOL resurfaces.

Billy has gained weight and muscle mass. His skin coloring casts a ruddy glow. All glaring remnants of self-inflicted wounds have healed. The scars from seizure-related incidents fade. His eyes are clear. His body movements are precise and coordinated. His stature exudes confidence. Whoever Billy meets, he extends his hand and looks them in the eye. He is not afraid. Billy knows what suffering means. Chronic conditions remain. The memories and the medical realities are part of his make-up. Yet whenever possible, Billy embraces life.

Improvisation

Blue and purple paint drips and pools on the canvass. The paint's flow varies depending on how Billy shifts the 48-by-48-inch piece. Even though it is large and unwieldy, Billy turns it with uninterrupted ease. His handling of his work is smooth, precise, and deliberate. Clad in a blue-jean painter apron stiffened with layers of paint, Billy stands a few feet away and observes. His eyes scan every brush stroke, every drip, every collision, every divide, and every unfolding. Nothing on the canvass is left unnoticed or unresolved.

The canvass rests on an oak easel with a shelf lip that is caked with years of vibrant paint run-off. No color dominates. Each hue is clear, hard, and evenly delineated on the wooden lip. After years of flicking and throwing paint, the white wall behind the easel is splattered with every color on the spectrum. The paint-laden wall is a masterpiece. The fluorescent lights overhead spotlight the swaths, spills, and smears of color throughout the studio.

Without hesitation, Billy reaches for two tools used to stir honey. Shaped like honeycombs, the carved wood spirals to a point. Dipping the tips into a plastic tub of cobalt blue paint, Billy twirls them so that the paint hovers in the crevices. In motionless flurry, Billy pivots and opens his body to face the canvass. His biceps flex and extend as each hand in unison creates floods and ripples of blue. Colors stream in all directions.

It appears that the art session is done. The cleanup routine begins. Billy drops the tools into a bucket of water. The CD player is turned off. The soulful wails of music cease. There are no more cues. There are no more directions. There are no more lessons. In this moment, however, there is a silence teeming with ideas. Stepping back up on the aerobic step to gain greater access to the canvass, Billy raises his left arm and stretches it forward to the right upper corner. His upper body twists as he delicately places his fingertips on the wet paint. His fingers caress the paint surface. Alert and steady, Billy's eyes rest deeply in sync with his creation. The direction he takes in the future is his to discover.

Afterword

By Christopher J. McDougle, MD
Director, Lurie Center for Autism
Professor of Psychiatry and Pediatrics,
Massachusetts General Hospital and
MassGeneral Hospital *for* Children
Nancy Lurie Marks Professor in the Field of Autism,
Harvard Medical School

A wake-up call is in order. Half a million children with autism will become adults in the next decade. Society at large, however, has not grasped the fact that autism is a lifelong disorder with comorbid medical illnesses. Thoughtful leaders in the field view autism not as an isolated neurological disease but as a systems disorder that likely has multiple potential causes including metabolic, immunological, genetic, and environmental.

The medical condition of individuals on the autism spectrum is often complex, yet poorly understood. If the word autism is mentioned to 100 people, 98 of them will likely see a child in their mind's eye. This and other statistics are sobering. Autism now affects one in 88 children. This fact combined with the number of young adults soon to turn 22 sets the stage for crisis on all medical fronts.

The current medical system is not prepared to provide healthcare for adults with autism. How is the medical community going to respond to the fast approaching, critical shortage of physicians trained to provide medical care for adults with autism? Stopgap measures will not suffice. Real changes are needed.

Medical schools and residency training programs need to develop and implement curricula on individuals with autism and other developmental disabilities across the lifespan. As part of standard medical evaluation, medical students are exposed to unique patient populations, including children, middle-aged adults, and the elderly. As the prevalence of autism and other developmental disabilities continues to increase, it may be time to require for medical students and residents comprehensive didactic learning and clinical rotations on developmental disabilities, including autism, across the lifespan.

Unless policymakers change the reimbursement schedules for the medical and psychiatric care of adults with autism and other developmental disabilities, medical students and other trainees will continue to receive the message that these individuals are not worth caring for and not valued by society. Physicians who complete specialty training in autism and other developmental disabilities should be compensated financially in line with other specialists. Otherwise, the result will continue to be that many adults with autism and other developmental disabilities will not have access to the same quality of medical care as many of us.

Advocacy, dialogue, and action can transform the inevitability of such abysmal outcomes. At Massachusetts General Hospital (MGH), concerned doctors, residents, nurses, therapists, administrators, and parents worked together and created a tool that supports patients with autism as well all the medical staff involved in their care. The Autism Care Questionnaire (ACQ) "provides medical staff with a quick and easy way to learn about a patient's communication methods, sensory differences and other potential stressors or safety concerns." MGH and the Lurie Center for Autism embarked upon a review of its policies and practices across the hospital. This initiative became known as the Autism Care Collaborative, which is an ongoing project. Currently administrative, communication, medical and education practices all are being evaluated and revised in light of the needs of adults on the autism spectrum.

Learning to Kiss is a unique account of how autism can awaken our sensitivity and deepen our understanding of the medical challenges that people living with this condition face, especially as they become adults. In this evocative memoir, Eve Megargel shatters our previously conceived notions about what constitutes the needs and desires of individuals with autism.

The rich and complex human impact of autism on adults and their families has yet to become part of the public consciousness. It is time to tell these stories. It is time to listen, learn, and understand. The stakes are too high not to respond.

Acknowledgments

To Matt – Our years of nightly phone conversations that involved my latest recitation of a story allowed me to hear my own voice in the midst of our shared lives. *Learning to Kiss* would not have been possible without your wisdom and abiding love.

To Ben – Your incisive edits, probing questions, and attention to the myriad of details at each stage of the process raised the bar of excellence. Your exemplary collaboration fueled my creative energies. Thank you for believing that Billy's story should be told.

To Billie Fitzpatrick, my editor – Your emphatic listening combined with your gracious invitation to explore other dimensions of the "story" deepened my understanding of and recall of those seminal human details.

To all those individuals who directly or indirectly have infused Billy's life and my own life with joy, compassion, humor, insights, and ultimately healing: I will always honor your diverse gifts.

Eve Megargel is an author, educator, filmmaker, and pioneer in advocating that all individuals on the autism spectrum are independent communicators who are capable of self-expression and social relationships. Eve consults, collaborates, and engages on key autism issues and initiatives with several organizations, including Massachusetts General Hospital and Boston's Jewish Family & Children's Service. She is a member of the MGH Family Advisory Council and the Lurie Leadership Council, an MGH subsidiary that works to "advance the clinical care and treatment of autism" for thousands of New England families. Her work at MGH led directly to the creation of the hospital's Autism Care Questionnaire (ACQ), which is designed to improve the experiences of patients with autism spectrum disorders when receiving medical services. Eve is currently participating in MGH's hospital-wide "Adults with Autism Initiative," which focuses on the medical, administrative, and informational needs of adult patients on the autism spectrum.

In 2005, Eve produced a film that chronicled her son Billy's journey to become an independent communicator using a voice-output computer. She has presented the film to many graduate and undergraduate classes as well as at the internationally known Ladders Conference. Eve was recently selected to speak at the Freedom Writers Foundation Symposium. In 2012, her article, "Autism and Hospitals: A Difficult Match," was published in the peer-review *Academic Pediatrics*.

Under Eve's guidance, her son Billy—who is completely non-verbal— has become an accomplished local artist. His abstract, Jackson Pollack-esque work has been written about in the *Boston Globe*, and exhibited at the Lurie Center, Lesley University, and several Boston-area Starbucks. Currently, Billy has permanent installations at the Lurie Center for Autism, Massachusetts General Hospital for Children as well as at Massachusetts General Hospital.

Eve received her master's degree in theology from Harvard University, and her bachelor's degree from the University of North Carolina-Chapel Hill. She lives with her husband Matt and son Billy in Weston, Massachusetts.

Painting by Billy Megargel – www.wmmartgallery.com

Cover design by Laurel Korn

Author photograph by Scott Metzger

For more information about *Learning to Kiss* – www.EveMegargel.com

For more information about the Voice Colors Communication Resource Model – www.voicecolors.org

51792775R00162

Made in the USA
Lexington, KY
06 May 2016